First World War
and Army of Occupation
War Diary
France, Belgium and Germany

38 DIVISION
Divisional Troops
Divisional Signal Company
8 December 1914 - 7 April 1919

WO95/2548/1

The Naval & Military Press Ltd
www.nmarchive.com
Published in association with The National Archives

Published by

The Naval & Military Press Ltd

Unit 10 Ridgewood Industrial Park,

Uckfield, East Sussex,

TN22 5QE England

Tel: +44 (0) 1825 749494

www.naval-military-press.com

www.nmarchive.com

This diary has been reprinted in facsimile from the original. Any imperfections are inevitably reproduced and the quality may fall short of modern type and cartographic standards.

© Crown Copyright
Images reproduced by permission of The National Archives, London, England, 2015.

Contents

Document type	Place/Title	Date From	Date To
Heading	WO95/2548/1		
Heading	38th Division Divl Engineers 38th Divl Signal Coy R.E. Dec 1915-May 1919		
Heading	38th Signal Vol I Dec 15 May 19		
War Diary	Winchester	02/12/1915	02/12/1915
War Diary	Havre	03/12/1915	04/12/1915
War Diary	Rouquetoire	05/12/1915	07/12/1915
War Diary	St Venant	20/12/1914	30/12/1914
War Diary	Rouquetoire	08/12/1914	19/12/1914
Heading	38th Signals Vol 2		
War Diary		03/01/1916	28/01/1916
Heading	38th Signals Vol 3		
War Diary		03/02/1916	28/02/1916
Diagram etc	Line Diagram of YCH		
Heading	38 Div Sig Coy Vol 4		
War Diary		01/03/1916	31/03/1916
War Diary		29/03/1916	31/03/1916
War Diary	Locon	01/04/1916	14/04/1916
War Diary	La Gorgue	17/04/1916	11/06/1916
War Diary	St Venant	12/06/1916	12/06/1916
War Diary	Roellecourt	15/06/1916	31/07/1916
Heading	War Diary Of 38th (Welsh) Divisional Signal Coy. August 1916. Vol 9		
War Diary		01/08/1916	31/08/1916
Heading	War Diary 38th Signal Coy R.E. September 1916 Vol 10		
War Diary		01/09/1916	30/09/1916
Heading	Original War Diary-October 1916 Signal Company Royal Engineers 38th (Welsh) Division 31-10-1916. Vol 11		
War Diary	St. Sixte	01/10/1916	31/10/1916
Heading	Original War Diary November 1916 38th Divisional Signal Coy Royal Engineers Vol 12		
War Diary	St. Sixte	01/11/1916	30/12/1916
Heading	Original War Diary 38th Signal C.R.E. January 1917 Vol 14		
War Diary	Esquelbecq	01/01/1917	10/01/1917
War Diary	St Sixte	15/01/1917	17/01/1917
War Diary	St Sixte	04/01/1917	09/01/1917
Heading	Original War Diary 38 Signal CRE 38 Division February 1917. Vol 15		
War Diary	St Sixte	00/02/1917	00/02/1917
Heading	Original War Diary March 1917 38th Signal C.R.E.		
War Diary	St Sixte	01/03/1917	30/03/1917
Heading	Original War Diary April 1917 38 Signal C.R.E. 38th Division Vol 17		
War Diary	St. Sixte	01/04/1917	28/04/1917
Heading	Original War Diary May 1917. Signal Coy Royal Engineers 38th (Welsh) Division 31.5.1917. Vol 18		
War Diary	St. Sixte	01/05/1917	22/05/1917

Type	Description	From	To
Heading	Original War Diary 38th Div Signal C.R.E. June 1917 30/1/17 Vol 19		
War Diary	St. Sixte	01/06/1917	29/06/1917
Heading	Original War Diary 38th Signal C.R.E. 38th Division July 1917. 31/8/17 Vol 20		
War Diary	Norrent Fontes	01/07/1917	31/07/1917
Heading	Original War Diary August 1917 38th Signal C.R.E. Vol 21		
War Diary		01/08/1917	31/08/1917
Heading	Original War Diary September 1917 38th Divnl Signal C.R.E.		
War Diary		01/09/1917	26/09/1917
War Diary	Croix Du Bac	00/10/1917	14/10/1917
War Diary	Croix Du Bac	01/11/1917	30/12/1917
War Diary	Merville	01/02/1918	25/02/1918
War Diary	Steenwerck	01/03/1918	31/03/1918
Heading	V. Corps. Third Army. War Diary 38th Divisional Signal Company, R.E. April 1918		
War Diary		01/04/1918	12/04/1918
War Diary		08/04/1918	30/08/1918
Heading	War Diary September 1918. 38th Divl. Signal C.R.E. Vol 34		
War Diary	High Wood S9b.8.8	01/09/1918	01/09/1918
War Diary	Les Boeufs	03/09/1918	11/09/1918
War Diary	Etricourt	11/09/1918	30/09/1918
Diagram etc	Typical Diagram Of Commns During Operations Of Sept. 1918		
War Diary	Near Fins.	02/10/1918	04/10/1918
War Diary	Epehy	04/10/1918	06/10/1918
War Diary	Hindenburg Line	06/10/1918	09/10/1918
War Diary	Villers Outreaux	10/10/1918	10/10/1918
War Diary	Bertry	11/10/1918	12/10/1918
War Diary	Clary	12/10/1918	22/10/1918
War Diary	K.25.d.7.4	24/10/1918	24/10/1918
War Diary	Montay	25/10/1918	25/10/1918
War Diary	Richemont	26/10/1918	31/10/1918
Miscellaneous	Addendum To Signal Arrangements. For 10-10-18	10/10/1918	10/10/1918
War Diary	Richmont	01/11/1918	03/11/1918
War Diary	Englefontaine	04/11/1918	05/11/1918
War Diary	Locquignol	06/11/1918	07/11/1918
War Diary	Aulnoye	08/11/1918	30/11/1918
War Diary	Aulnoye	29/11/1918	29/12/1918
War Diary	Inchy	30/12/1918	30/12/1918
War Diary	Glisy	31/12/1918	14/01/1919
War Diary	Querrieu	14/01/1919	01/04/1919
War Diary	Glisy	07/04/1919	00/05/1919

WO95/25481

38TH DIVISION
DIVL ENGINEERS

38TH DIVL SIGNAL COY R.E.
DEC 1915 – MAY 1919

38th Federal
2 Vol I

Dec 15
nov 19

38th Divl Signal Co. R.E.

WAR DIARY
or
INTELLIGENCE SUMMARY

Army Form C. 2118.

(Erase heading not required.)

Instructions regarding War Diaries and Intelligence Summaries are contained in F. S. Regs., Part II. and the Staff Manual respectively. Title pages will be prepared in manuscript.

Place	Date	Hour	Summary of Events and Information	Remarks and references to Appendices
Winchester	1915 Dec 2	9.0 am	Headquarters, No 1, and 3 Sections proceeded by road from Winchester to Southampton for France. Service. Arrived at Southampton 3.0 pm. The following mishaps occurred during the journey:— 6023 Dvr A. Clarke sustained an injury to his foot caused by a horse falling on him. A cart wheel passed over the heel of 63028 Sapper R.H. Williams. Embarkation was completed at 11.4.5 pm.	
	3 Dec		Arrived at Havre, disembarked, & proceeded to Rest Camp No 5. Sapper R.H. Williams & Driver A. Clarke remained at Havre & were sent to No 2 Hospital in accordance with Embarkation Officers instructions.	

38th Divisional Signal Company.

WAR DIARY
or
INTELLIGENCE SUMMARY.

Army Form C. 2118.

Place	Date	Hour	Summary of Events and Information	Remarks and references to Appendices
HAVRE	4 Dec		Proceeded from HAVRE by train, motor lorry in charge of Sergeant	
Rougestemes - 5 Dec			COLLINS proceeded by road. arrived at BLENDECQUES, and after detraining marched to ROUGEFTOIRE. Arranged billets with Interpreter & established Signal office.	
	6 Dec		Established Communication with 113th 114th and 115th Infantry Brigades. Also R.G. cables to 113th Brigade. Motor lorry in charge of Sergt COLLINS arrived 9.0 am. Visited 1st Army Signals at AIRE and the 46th Division at ST.	
	7 Dec		VENANT. Lateral communication between Infantry Brigades established, and Brigades were engaged in establishing communication with their Battalions. 1st Army Signals established line to Divisional Headquarters. A.D.M.S. connected by telephone. Pro. D. Daniels etc.	

Army Form C. 2118.

WAR DIARY
or
INTELLIGENCE SUMMARY.
(Erase heading not required.)

Instructions regarding War Diaries and Intelligence Summaries are contained in F. S. Regs., Part II. and the Staff Manual respectively. Title pages will be prepared in manuscript.

Place	Date	Hour	Summary of Events and Information	Remarks and references to Appendices
St Venant	Dec 20th 1914		Moved to St Venant; laid lines to brigades.	
	Dec 23rd 1914		Changed 115th Brigade line from cable to permanent line. Capt H.P. JESSON arrived from 1st Army Signals. R.E.	
	Dec 24th		Capt S. BOWYER left for 1st Army Signals and Capt Jesson assumed command. Line laid from CRA to 119 Bde R.F.A.	
	Dec 26th		Lieut E.F. BACON, R.E. (T.C.) arrived as supernumerary officer from 1st Army Signals. Hours of relief changed to 8am, 1:30pm, 5:30pm & 10pm instead of 8 hours on 16 off.	
	Dec 27th		CRA connected to 121st & 122nd Bdes RFA on one line using D3 telephones.	
	Dec 28th		CRA connected to 120th Bde R.F.A. (D3 telephone cable)	
	Dec 29th		Above line produced to divl. ammn. col. Sergeant Williams & Cpl Williamson joined unit to be temporarily attached as instructors.	
	Dec 30th		SC Dis train connected to exchange. Classes in cable drill started.	

H.P. Jesson
CAPT RE
OC 38th Div Signal Co RE.

5/1/16

Army Form C. 2118.

38th Divisional War Diary Company R.E. 3

WAR DIARY
or
INTELLIGENCE SUMMARY.
(Erase heading not required.)

Place	Date	Hour	Summary of Events and Information	Remarks and references to Appendices
Rouspetres	8 Dec		Lt Col. J. Godfrey-Fawcett arrived from 1st Army H.Q. and made some useful suggestions. 115th Brigade line gave trouble and linesmen were sent out to improve laying & to locate faults. Telephonic communication established with C.R.E., d.a.d.s.t., and A.D.V.S. 113th Brigade reported D.1. Cable used up & enamelled cable gave trouble owing to being too brittle for successful use.	
	9th Dec		Line laid to CRE	
	12th Dec		Line laid to CRA	
	13th Dec		Lines laid to artillery Brigades and Divisional Ammunition Column	
	18th Dec		Artillery lines reeled in	
	19th Dec		Infantry Brigade and local lines reeled in.	

38ª Spinalo
vol 2

WAR DIARY or INTELLIGENCE SUMMARY.

Army Form C. 2118.

(Erase heading not required.)

Place	Date	Hour	Summary of Events and Information	Remarks and references to Appendices
	3/1/16		4 men from RFA attached for instruction in cable laying, fault finding etc. Changed over line CRA - 121 Bde RFA - 122 Bde RFA from cable to comic airline.	
	4/1/16		Changed over line CRA - 120 Bde RFA - DAC from cable to comic airline.	
	5/1/16		Shifted billet for mounted men & horses, as the farm we were in was required as a rest store.	
	6/1/16		Laid comic airline to CRA for metallic telephone circuit.	
	7/1/16		Shifted billet again, the last one being required for cultivator purposes. Electric light installed in signal office from town supply.	
	8/1/16		Laid comic airline to 119 Bde RFA in place of cable.	
	9/1/16		Took over lines laid by 1st Army Signals to Colonne's Les Laurieres tons of our brigade headquarters. 2328 Sgt R. Tait from DO Cable section attached a/c SM vice a/c SM Marks who recorded to 5 scrip to his own request.	

Army Form C. 2118.

WAR DIARY
or
INTELLIGENCE SUMMARY.
(Erase heading not required.)

Instructions regarding War Diaries and Intelligence Summaries are contained in F. S. Regs., Part II. and the Staff Manual respectively. Title pages will be prepared in manuscript.

Place	Date	Hour	Summary of Events and Information	Remarks and references to Appendices
	10-1-16		Signal Office & Company office inspected by G.O.C. & G.S.O.I.	
	16-1-16		Sent 4 linesmen to new area to learn the lines.	
	17-1-16		D.A.S. & A.D.A.S. visited Headquarters & stayed to lunch.	
	22-1-16		G.O.C. 38th Division inspected wagons, horses, harness, billets & examined officers & men & all he saw in a letter to the C.R.E.	
	23-1-16		Sent forward one relief to listen.	
	24-1-16		Closed at St Venant at 10am (reopening) Listen at same hour, no hitch anywhere in spite of shortage of instruments.	
	26-1-16		Sent 1 N.C.O, 3 telegraphists & 3 R.E. exchange operators to learn procedure in O.R.P's office prior to taking over.	
	27-1-16		Detached 1 N.C.O & 4 men to Left Brigade to straighten cables in trenches.	
	29-1-16		Took over C.R.A's office.	

5 2/16

H. Menn
Capt R.E.
O.C. 38th Signal Co. R.E.

38th Signals
Vol: 3

Army Form C. 2118.

WAR DIARY 38th Signal Coy

INTELLIGENCE SUMMARY.

(Erase heading not required.)

Place	Date	Hour	Summary of Events and Information	Remarks and references to Appendices
	3rd Feb 1916		Started school for battalion operators (2 per battalion). Class to last 4 weeks & to include Buzzer operating, Office routine & care & theory of instruments. L/Cpl Williams in charge with one operator to help him. Hours :— 9-11 Buzzer 11-12 Lecture, 12-1 Buzzer, 2-4 Buzzer & short lecture.	
	5th Feb		Started replacing lines of right group R.A. with comic airline; one officer & 4 NCOs & men from this unit remainder of party from R.A. After 3 days the R.A. were able to carry on without help & they appeared very well satisfied with the new lines to say nothing of the cable they were able to recover.	
	6th Feb		Tested a drum of D6 cable to see if it laid well. Reported on as rather heavy but otherwise all right. Left the cable with a brigade section, who are to lay it in the front line for further test.	
	9th Feb		Started leading in lines to proposed new report centre at Vieille-Chapelle. Heard in evening that Division was to ride slip to the South. Completed "brick-on-edge" standing for half the horses in the unit.	

Army Form C. 2118.

WAR DIARY
or
INTELLIGENCE SUMMARY.
(Erase heading not required.)

Instructions regarding War Diaries and Intelligence Summaries are contained in F. S. Regs., Part II. and the Staff Manual respectively. Title pages will be prepared in manuscript.

Place	Date	Hour	Summary of Events and Information	Remarks and references to Appendices
	10th Feb 1916		Ruled up previous days report-centre work; visited 2nd Div Signals, who gave me a rough diagram of his lines, both a promise of a complete one if we should move into his area.	
	11th Feb 1916		Reconnoitred routes for our lines in expected new area. Collected poles from forests; prepared pegs & stays.	
	12th Feb 1916		Reconstructed 3 existing comic circuits LOCON to LOISNE; constructed fresh line LOCON – CENSE DU RAUX.	
	13th Feb 1916		Constructed line LOCON – LACOUTURE. Arranged with adc 1st Army for Sigs for him to construct a pair of wires from LOCON – CANAL JUNCTION for right Bde; a pair LOCON – CENSE DU RAUX for left Bde & a pair LACOUTURE – LOISNE for RA Groups at former place.	
	14th Feb 1916.		1st Corps Signals give us telephone pair to 33rd Div in Bethune; arrange with Sigs 33rd D W for direct buzzer line between our respective report centres. Start(s)laying in at LOCON & constructed another line LOCON – LOISNE.	

WAR DIARY
or
INTELLIGENCE SUMMARY.
(Erase heading not required.)

Army Form C. 2118.

Place	Date	Hour	Summary of Events and Information	Remarks and references to Appendices
	15th Feb 1916		Leading in at LOCON & LOISNE also putting through an existing airline HALTE-LOISNE. Arranged with 11th Corps Signals for two 4 bracket arms to be run through town of LOCON for local circuits.	
	16th Feb		Extending telephone bar' LOISNE-JACOUTURE to 119 Bde RFA, who are apparently not going to move.	
	17th Feb		Improving lines & leading in.	
	18th Feb		Moved to LOCON. Lines as per attached diagram viz; telephone & morse to each Bde. Two trunks to LOISNE exchange whence can get all Bdes Inf & Art; telephone to side divs & left div RA from LOISNE. Telephone & morse to Corps.	
	19th Feb		CRA moved to LOISNE.	
	20th Feb		Laid lines to 105 Bde & 119 Bde RFA both arriving at short notice near LOCON, former joined to Div exchange latter to RA exchange. Also put through line from 35th Div Exchange to 2nd Indian Bde RHA just arrived at FOSSE & attached 38th Div.	

Army Form C. 2118.

WAR DIARY
or
INTELLIGENCE SUMMARY.
(Erase heading not required.)

Instructions regarding War Diaries and Intelligence Summaries are contained in F. S. Regs., Part II. and the Staff Manual respectively. Title pages will be prepared in manuscript.

Place	Date	Hour	Summary of Events and Information	Remarks and references to Appendices
	20th Feb 1916		O.C. took over new area from 2nd D. so enabling us to discard 2nd Div lines from LOISNE exchange. Substitute our own.	
	21st Feb		Fixed up lines at LOISNE where there was some confusion as owing to the telephone exchange being moved from Groups HQ to Bde HQ.	
	22nd Feb		Connected RE Stow & 123 W.Bgde Fd Co to exchange.	
	23rd Feb		Connected 124 Fd Co to same line as 123 Fd Co.	
	26th Feb		Joined pigeon loft LA COUTURE to Brigadier to tel. group.	
			Changed our local circuits from cable to permanent line constructed by Corps.	
	27th Feb		Connected DDC to CRA's exchange.	
	28th Feb		Started constructing new horse standings.	

AM Jesson
..................Capt. R. E.
O.C. 38th Signal Co. R. E.

7/3/16

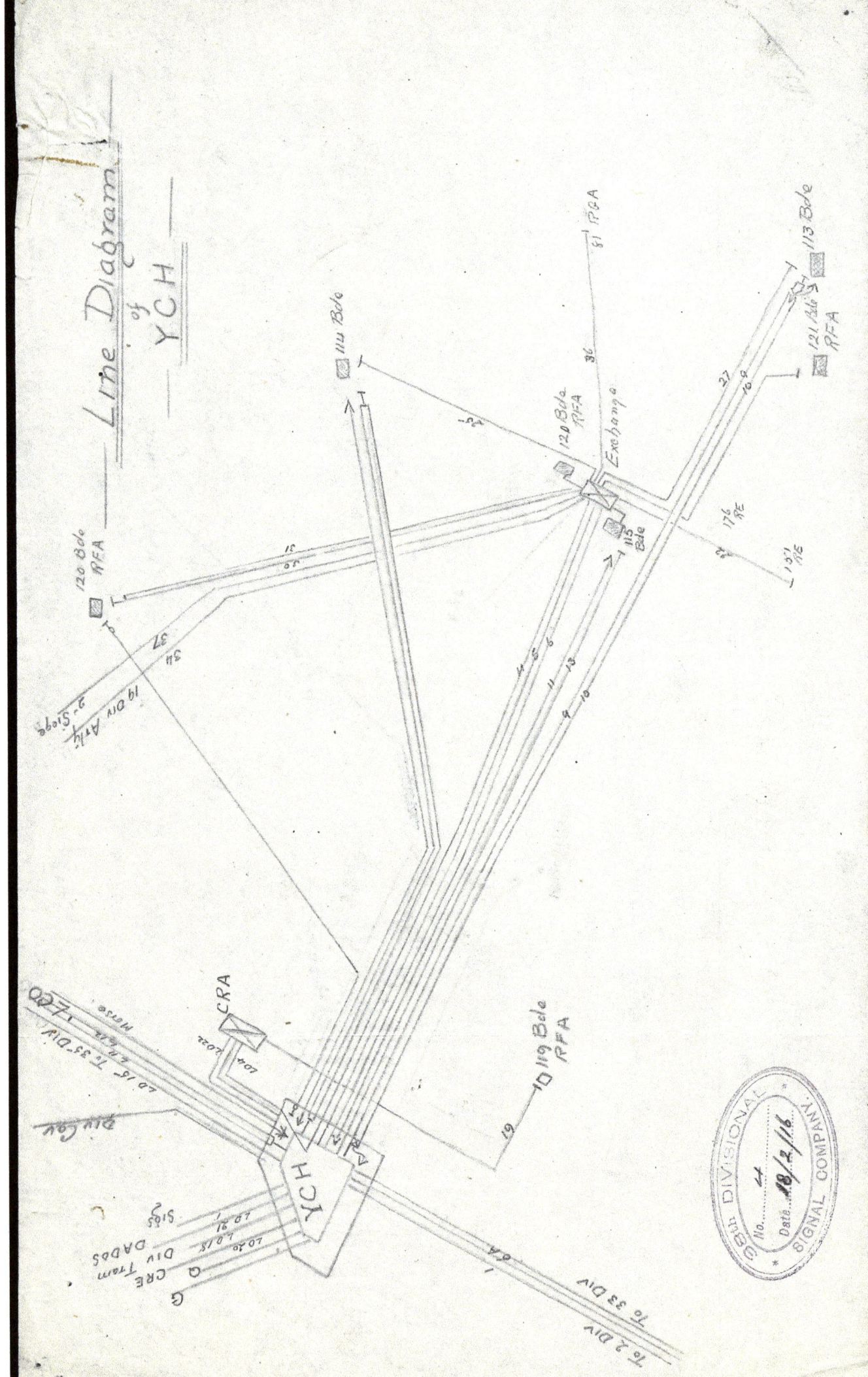

38 Div
Sig Coy
Vol. 4

38 Sig Coy

WAR DIARY
INTELLIGENCE SUMMARY
(Erase heading not required.)

Army Form C. 2118.

Place	Date	Hour	Summary of Events and Information	Remarks and references to Appendices
	1.3.16		Laid comic line to new position for Reserve Brigade	
	2.3.16		Trouble with horses owing to mud. Cracked heels, skin trouble & kicks. Put 1 N.C.O. in charge of sick horses & hastened construction of brick standings.	
	3.3.16		Bathing & fetching slag for horse standings.	
	4.3.16		Tidied up lines at Report Centre.	
	6.3.16		Improving billet area.	
	7.3.16		XI Corps moved to HINGES from MERVILLE. Reeled up B wire route BETHUNE-HALTE given in by 1st Corps, material 9 bracket arms, P.O. insulators & rough H poles. Started line to D.A.C. at MONT BERNECHON.	
	8.3.16		Completed line to D.A.C. (earth return comic). Replaced Bable Lewis C.R.A. – 119 Bde R.F.A. & LOISNE – R.E. Coys with comic.	
	9.3.16		Bathing. Visited 120 Bde R.F.A. & pigeon loft in LAQUUTURE	
	10.3.16		Reeled up comic line LOCON – CENSE-DURAUX. Laid comic LOISNE – RUE DU BOIS.	

Army Form C. 2118.

WAR DIARY
or
INTELLIGENCE SUMMARY.
(Erase heading not required.)

Place	Date	Hour	Summary of Events and Information	Remarks and references to Appendices
	11.3.16		Replaced cable in LOISNE – CENSE DU RAUX line with conic	
	12.3.16		Reeled up cable LOISNE – LE TOURET. Completed metallic circuits CRA – LOISNE y BWHQ – LOISNE y changed over from single wires.	
	13.3.16		Visited 4 batteries in centre group.	
	16.3.16		Second trunk to LOISNE made metallic. New labelling system issued.	
	17.3.16		Started morse line to Right Bde. to do away with transformers. Test party to Left Brigade to lay second line from Companies to Battalions to be kept plugged through to RA for use as S.O.S. lines. Struck lath in Bethune to make bearings for motor cycle, which cannot be obtained from Supply Column; 4 machines out of action for want of them.	
	18.3.16		Completed line to right brigade. Visited night party laying Battalion – Company lines. Beautiful moonlight night & very peaceful both sides intent on improving their defences. Completed horse standings; trucks on edge for all horses, as had conv.	

Army Form C. 2118.

WAR DIARY
or
INTELLIGENCE SUMMARY.
(Erase heading not required.)

Instructions regarding War Diaries and Intelligence Summaries are contained in F.S. Regs., Part II. and the Staff Manual respectively. Title pages will be prepared in manuscript.

Place	Date	Hour	Summary of Events and Information	Remarks and references to Appendices
	19.3.16		Bathing, rifle etc inspection.	
	20.3.16		Started new telephone route to right bde to replace civilian. Material from B wing route picked up on 7th inst stout rough poles, short arms, P.O. insulators. Route march for 1B section 13 miles.	
	21.3.16		Completed telephone route to Right Bde leaving civilians above. Arranged with Corps for there & others to be relied in.	
	22.3.16		255 Co RE at LE HAMEL connected to OISNE exchange. Fenny Signal II Lieut R.B. LISTER arrived from RE arrangements to be attached for instruction.	
			Replaced centrifuga at telephone line with new metallic circuit.	
	24.3.16		120 Bde RFA been forwarded a room back to rest. Joined to CRA exchange	
	25.3.16		Making test pole on RUE DU BOIS. Bathing & inspections of kit.	
	26.3.16		Trouble on DAC line where it ran on permanent poles along canal. Some enemy had been bombing along the reserve trenches alongside telephone route. Wires down for about 600 yds. Matter reported to staff.	

2353 Wt. W2544/1454 700,000 5/15 D. D. & L. A.D.S.S./Forms/C. 2118.

Army Form C. 2118.

WAR DIARY
or
INTELLIGENCE SUMMARY.
(Erase heading not required.)

Instructions regarding War Diaries and Intelligence Summaries are contained in F. S. Regs., Part II. and the Staff Manual respectively. Title pages will be prepared in manuscript.

Place	Date	Hour	Summary of Events and Information	Remarks and references to Appendices
	29/3/16		Visited GIVENCHY area, Lines requiring straightening. Arranged for men & material.	
	30.3.16		D.W. Suffolks Column hut in exchange. Messages previously sent though D.O. on our left who had a brigade in same village. The brigade having left better communication necessary.	
	31/3/16		Assisted R.A. to replace cable lines with cover. We now have no cable out behind brigades & only one short length of airline. All lines are covered, which works well, though lines require much attention at this time of year owing to stay pegs being ploughed up.	

M Jesson
Capt RE.
31/3/16. OC 38 Signal Co RE.

WAR DIARY
or
INTELLIGENCE SUMMARY.
(Erase heading not required.)

Army Form C. 2118.

Place	Date	Hour	Summary of Events and Information	Remarks and references to Appendices
	29.3.16		Visited GIVENCHY area, huts require straightening. Arranged for men & material.	
	30.3.16		D.U Supply Column put in exchange. Messages previously sent through Div on our left who had a brigade in same village. The brigade having left better communication necessary.	
	31.3.16		Assisted R.A. to replace cable line with conduit. We now have no cables out behind brigades & only one short length of airline. All lines are conduit, which works well, though lines require much attention at this time of year owing to stays pegs being ploughed up.	

Messon
Capt R.E.

31/3/16.   OC 38 Signal Co R.E.

Signals
Army Form C. 2118.
38/24
VI5

WAR DIARY

INTELLIGENCE SUMMARY.

(Erase heading not required.) 38th Signal Co.

Instructions regarding War Diaries and Intelligence Summaries are contained in F. S. Regs., Part II. and the Staff Manual respectively. Title pages will be prepared in manuscript.

Place	Date	Hour	Summary of Events and Information	Remarks and references to Appendices
LOCON	1.4.16		A Section route march with horses etc end.	
	2.4.16		Built cable line LOISNE towards LOCON aio farco canal to replace cableline.	
	3.4.16		Started linesman's class under CSM Tait. Class consisting of 2 men per Co. See. Course based on qualification sheet, consisting of ridings, cable & cableline, pole climbing & instruments.	
	4.4.16		Constructed riding school for use of linesman's class.	
	6.4.16		Started building cable lines from Reserve Brigade to its battalions to replace cable laid out.	
	7.4.16		3rd course for battalion signallers commenced. Inspection of horses by DDVS 1st Army.	
	10.4.16		Completed cable line from Reserve Bde to battalions. Started daily drill for officers relief, who march very badly.	
	12.4.16		2/Lieut C.A.C. Aitkens 3/1st S. Midland S&C. arrived for 14 days course of instruction.	
	13.4.16		Put through 2 lines LA GORGUE — LAVENTIE for use in new area. Sent forward NCO & 3 men to new area to learn lines.	

Army Form C. 2118.

WAR DIARY
or
INTELLIGENCE SUMMARY.
(Erase heading not required.)

Instructions regarding War Diaries and Intelligence Summaries are contained in F.S. Regs., Part II and the Staff Manual respectively. Title pages will be prepared in manuscript.

Place	Date	Hour	Summary of Events and Information	Remarks and references to Appendices
LOCON	14.4.16		115 Bde at Estaires joined to 19 Div exchange at LA GORGUE. Line put through from 19th Bde R.A. to LAVENTIE for use of our left group RA.	
LA GORGUE	17.4.16		Moved to LA GORGUE took over from 19 Bk Div, MOATED GRANGE, NEUVE CHAPELLE & FME DU BOIS sectors. Lines in former in bad condition.	
	19.4.16		Much manure to be carted in H.Q. (billet). Party to 113 Bde to assist in tidying lines. Extended DAC line to new HR.	
	20.4.16		Gave up NEUVE CHAPELLE FME DU BOIS sectors & took over FAUQUISSART sector; latter has good lines. Extended old 19 Div Train line to MERVILLE Civil exchange.	
	22.4.16		Discontinued party with 113 Bde as pronounced unsafe & returned to supply columns.	
	23.4.16		EASTER DAY – Church Parade & no work.	
	25.4.16		Installed exchange at COCKSHY HOUSE – LAVENTIE. Right bde H.Q. Lines to D.W.H.Q. 123,124,151 Fd Cos RE, 19 Pioneer Btln. R.V.L Bdes.	

2353 Wt. W2514/1454 700,000 5/15 D.D.& L. A.D.S.S./Forms/C. 2118.

Army Form C. 2118.

WAR DIARY
or
INTELLIGENCE SUMMARY.
(Erase heading not required.)

Instructions regarding War Diaries and Intelligence Summaries are contained in F. S. Regs., Part II. and the Staff Manual respectively. Title pages will be prepared in manuscript.

Place	Date	Hour	Summary of Events and Information	Remarks and references to Appendices
	25.4.16		Completed 3 conic lines from R.A. office to R v L. Groups v 122 Bde R.F.A. Previously lines to these ran along permanent routes.	
	26.4.16		Connected R.E. store to adv exchange. 2 Lieut Aitken left.	
	27.4.16		Altered lines to reserve Bde giving them one phone in staff room v one in signal office. All bdes now have this.	
	28.4.16		1a Lined NCO v 4 men to Right bde for several days	
	30.4.16		Inspected lineman's class on completion of course.	

J P Jesson
Capt RE
OC 38th Signal Co RE

30/4/16

38 Div
Signals
Vol 6

Army Form C. 2118.

WAR DIARY
INTELLIGENCE SUMMARY.
(Erase heading not required.)

Place	Date	Hour	Summary of Events and Information	Remarks and references to Appendices
LA GORGUE	1.5.16		Continued party of 1 NCO & 4 men with high tide (MOATED GRANGE sector) to assist in tidying lines in trenches. 5 men from linemen's class selected for further instruction.	
	3.5.16		Assisted B battery 119 bde to build a comic line to their wagon lines. 2nd Lieut A. GRIST 60th Signal Co arrived for 7 days attachment. 3rd class of battalion operators closed.	
	5.5.16		Comic airline constructed between R & L bdes to replace cable.	
	6.5.16		Cable from adv exchange to 19th Pioneers & 151 Co RE replaced by comic on permanent poles.	
	7.5.16		Connected R. Group R.A. to 18 Anti aircraft section at request of CRA. 4th class of battalion operators commenced.	
	8.5.16		6 Cyclist & 4 mounted orderlies attached from Cyclist Co & Div mounted troops returned to their units. Started 2 relief system, the 3rd relief providing cyclist orderlies. Replaced cable in lines Adv Exchange to 123 & 124 Cos RE with comic. Linemen's class closed	

WAR DIARY

INTELLIGENCE SUMMARY.

Army Form C. 2118.

Place	Date	Hour	Summary of Events and Information	Remarks and references to Appendices
LAGORGUE	10.5.16	—	Commenced inspection of lines to see that they were safe & properly labelled. I Lieut Instrument home.	
	11.5.16	—	Inspection continued.	
	12.5.16	—	Inspection completed and report sent to staff. Although divisional lines are very well laid & labelled on the whole suggest following precautions (1) That no D1 cable be used in danger area. (2) That metallic circuits must be composed of same class of cable of same age laid side by side or twisted. (3) That all single lines in danger area be reeled up unchi my orders after a certain date. DDAS visited brigades.	
	13.5.16		I NCO & I man to assist R.A in tidying up lines outside O.P's. A cable Section of XI Corps start reeling up spare cables in S. TILLELOY ST Lieut EF Bacon appointed temp Capt whilst 2nd in command from 27-2-16 Started burying lines entering R. Bde HdQrs.	
	14.5.16			

Army Form C. 2118.

WAR DIARY
or
INTELLIGENCE SUMMARY.
(Erase heading not required.)

Place	Date	Hour	Summary of Events and Information	Remarks and references to Appendices
LA GORGUE	16.5.16		Work much hindered by having to provide cycle orderlies since 8.5.16. The 2 relief system appears to work very well.	
	17.5.16		ADAS VI Corps visited brigades & front line.	
	21.5.16		A Linemen's class for infantry signallers assembled consisting of 1 man per battalion. Objects (1) to impress on men necessity of careful line maintenance. (2) Instruction in laying, jointing, maintaining lines. (3) Assisting brigades in keeping forward area clear. (4) Reeling up spare lines & unsafe lines in forward area.	
	22.5.16		Comic line for R.A. constructed.	
	23.5.16		Started 4 line comic to LAVENTIE.	
	24.5.16		Continued comic line to LAVENTIE	
	25.5.16		Capt Jeavon proceeded on leave to U.K. Capt Beer took over. Route inspected for scheme of buried cable GorGoe HQ to Cols Bde HQ. 2/Lt Hemmington & four men arrived for course of instruction in line	
	26.5.16		Relay Comic Route in way to Right & Left Bdes. Started buried cable at Right Bde HQ. 8 Galob. H. mounted men (Westmorland & Cumberland Yeomanry) for duty as orderlies.	

Army Form C. 2118.

WAR DIARY
or
INTELLIGENCE SUMMARY.
(Erase heading not required.)

Instructions regarding War Diaries and Intelligence Summaries are contained in F.S. Regs., Part II. and the Staff Manual respectively. Title pages will be prepared in manuscript.

Place	Date	Hour	Summary of Events and Information	Remarks and references to Appendices
LA GORGUE	27.5.16		Went to my Coms Route to Right & to Left Bdes	
			Recking up Callis in forward area	
	28.5.16		Visited ADs XI Corps for conference	
			Returned & Germany who reported here on 25.5.11 back to H Coy Regt	
			to others reported for duty from same Regt	
	29.5.16		Luting up Route held by Corps sgs to Bdes to any points to meet	
			buried cable test box	
	30.5.16		Prepared buried cable Left Bde	
	31.5.16		Visited by ADas X Corps	
			2 Lieut G. Martineau arrived for 7 days attachment from XI Corps signal	
			Lieut D P Jones 60th (West) Division (T) arrived for 7 days attachment	

2/6/16

E. J. Bacon Capt RE
38 Division Signal Coy

38. Div Signals

WAR DIARY
or
INTELLIGENCE SUMMARY.

Army Form C. 2118.

Vol 7

Place	Date	Hour	Summary of Events and Information	Remarks and references to Appendices
LA GORGUE	1/6/16		2nd Lieut Marshand proceeded to 113 Bde for instruction. Completed bringing of divisional lines into Left Bde HQ. Changed over Right Bde lines to new route, strengthened same.	
	3/6/16		Built a 2 line route from advanced exchange LAVENTIE to position of Australian Tunnelling Co at LE DRUMEZ; latter place also report centre of Reserve Bde. Inspection of wagons by D.A.D.O.S. Extending one leg of above to Div Bomb Store.	
	4/6/16			
	5/6/16		Operators class returned to units. Rising all lines across railway in Div area. 2 Line parties from R. Group RA, LAVENTIE to Railway Sta.	
	6/6/16		Clearing up lines at LAVENTIE.	
	7/6/16		Driving drill 2 teams per section. New operators class commenced, 2 men per battalion as before.	
	11/6/16		Put through 2 lines ST VENANT to ROBECQ in anticipation of move to former place.	
ST VENANT	12.6.16		Moved ST VENANT	

Army Form C. 2118.

WAR DIARY
or
INTELLIGENCE SUMMARY.
(Erase heading not required.)

Instructions regarding War Diaries and Intelligence Summaries are contained in F. S. Regs., Part II. and the Staff Manual respectively. Title pages will be prepared in manuscript.

Place	Date	Hour	Summary of Events and Information	Remarks and references to Appendices
STIVENANT	14.6.16		Lieut R.D. SHERGOLD, 113 Bde Signal Section evacuated home sick. 2nd Lieut F.V. PEARSON takes 113 Bde v Capt E.F. BACON 1 B. Section. Advance party 2 NCOs & 3 men to ROELLE COURT. Time advanced 1 hour at 11 p.m.	
ROELLE COURT	15.6.16		Moved ROELLE COURT men St Pol for training under XVII Corps. 3rd Army.	
	16.6.16		Signalling scheme to Corps (7miles). By visual. Successful except for 1 NCO. Lecture on map reading.	
	17.6.16		1A Cable drill; remainder Infantry drill	
	18.6.16		ditto ditto	
			1 officer & 4 O.R. from H.Q. & Nos 2 & 4 Secs attend 2 days course at 13 Sqdn R.F.C. for instruction in signalling to aeroplanes.	
	19.6.16		1B Cable drill remainder infantry drill visual. Shifted horse lines for fear of infection.	
	20.6.16		Work as for 19th.	

Army Form C. 2118.

WAR DIARY
or
INTELLIGENCE SUMMARY.
(Erase heading not required.)

Instructions regarding War Diaries and Intelligence Summaries are contained in F. S. Regs., Part II and the Staff Manual respectively. Title pages will be prepared in manuscript.

Place	Date	Hour	Summary of Events and Information	Remarks and references to Appendices
ROELLECOURT	21/6/16		1B v 1B visual signallers testscheme with R.A. Research drill.	
	22.6.16		1A Signal scheme, usual by HQ detachment — " —	
	23.6.16		Signal scheme detachments from 1A, 1B Sqn visual from HQ — " —	
	24.6.16		Laying lines for Divisional scheme.	
	25.6.16		Divisional scheme.	
	26.6.16		Moved LE MEILLARD.N. of DOULLENS included II Corps. Morse to Corps.	
	27/6/16		Superimposed telephone to Corps. Delay thru fault in DOULLENS Office.	
	28/6/16		Laid lines to Brigades v CRP. 2 Lines in all at atg 8/p.m. Installed exchange G.Q. Corps direct Brigades v CRA through commutator.	
	29/6/16		Improved Brigade lines.	
	30/6/16		Advance party to RUBEMPRE. Scheme with 9 Sqdn RFC cooperation between Inf & Aeroplanes. Received 8 cyclists from Corps.	

JPJesson
.... Capt., R. E.
O.C. 38th Signal Co. R. E.

30/6/16

Army Form C. 2118.

WAR DIARY
or
INTELLIGENCE SUMMARY.
(Erase heading not required.)

38 Divn
Signals

Place	Date	Hour	Summary of Events and Information	Remarks and references to Appendices
	July 1916			
	1st	6.30	Closed office at Le Meillard & reopened at Rubempré same hour	
			Reeled up Brigade S.R.A. lines at Le Meillard	
	2nd		Marched from Rubempré to Leal Villers	
			Closed reopened office 10.0 a.m	
	3rd		Closed at Leal Villers at 7.30 p.m reopened at Treux	
	4th		Overhaul of wagon stores	
	5th			
	6th		Moved to Grove Town N/ Bray took over from 7 Div at 6.0 p.m. Received orders at 10 p.m that 113 Bde were moving to advanced Report Centre Cpl Bacon & party started off at 8.15 p.m. Laid Cable direct from Div to 113 Bde 5 miles though at 5.0 a.m. Received line laid by Stg 6 Divn to same place though at 8.0 a.m. extent 33 Divn S/R 113 Bde moved to near position this extended	
	7th		Laid cable to Caterpillar Wood but shot away as soon as laid repaired several times but line was cut as soon as repaired Bad weather set in trouble with buried lines Laid new line forward in trenches area to 115 Bde Communication by telegraph telephone	

290 a/forms 290 C/9 Divnl D R.

2353 Wt. W2514/1454 700,000 5/15 D. D. & L. A.D.S.S./Forths/C. 2118.

Army Form C. 2118.

WAR DIARY
or
INTELLIGENCE SUMMARY.
(Erase heading not required.)

Instructions regarding War Diaries and Intelligence Summaries are contained in F.S. Regs., Part II. and the Staff Manual respectively. Title pages will be prepared in manuscript.

Place	Date	Hour	Summary of Events and Information	Remarks and references to Appendices
	July 8th		Laid direct line from Div HQ to Report Centre of 113 Bde	
		2.0 am	Lain from Test Station to divide final at 2nd Hackham from divns line to 115 Bde Copr Baen from 115 Bde to Report Centre in Danzig Alley, also line Danzig Alley to Pommiers redoubt line 7 miles. Telegraph to three Bdes. 329 afms 260 C forms 34 Special D.R's.	
	9th		Tested line to 122 Bde R.F.A. in Mametz – Fricourt Rd via Ville thenet. Handed over communications to O.C Signals guarnison who still worked with 36 Div staff Telegraph to two Bdes. 275 Afms 215 C forms 41 Special D.R's	
			7 Invain working officer Orc Bde on Telegraph 270 Afms 230 C forms 1 Special D.R's	
	10		Handed over to 21st Division at 6.0 pm. Stayed at Treus same town. 8 Special D.R's	
	11		Moved from Treus 6.0 pm with Div Train to Coray arrived 1.0 am (15 miles) 3 Special D.R's	
	12		Left Coray 7.0 am arrived Port-Remy 11.30 pm (30 miles)	
	13		Rested & overhauled stores	
	14			

WAR DIARY
or
INTELLIGENCE SUMMARY

Army Form C. 2118.

(Erase heading not required.)

Place	Date	Hour	Summary of Events and Information	Remarks and references to Appendices
	July 1916 15.		Left Pont Remy at 4.0 am reached Corin at 10.30 pm (140 miles)	
	16.		Closed office. Pilot Party of reformed at Corin at 11.0 am. Coy noted linemen on new lines. 2nd Brigr left by a. & G. to help with buried lines system.	
	17		2nd Davis checking all stores on cable sections. Horse inspection by A.D.V.S.	
	18		Party reforming 7 way route Corin - Sell. Labelling lines in Sug pits	
	19		Party reforming route to Sell Exchange, 10 line exchange installed giving second way to Bde.	
	20		Party building line Div HQ to Res Bde at Sell. Res Div dump party on telep line, repaired Right Div line	
	21		Party raising wires behind Sell Exchange, working out buried leads in N up Sug axis.	
	22		Laid line from Sell Exchange to 114 Bde. Baths for 100 men.	
	23.		Reconstruction of Trunk to Sell. 2nd Haslam working out lines in A.B.L. & Div axis for connecting Dragons.	

Army Form C. 2118.

WAR DIARY
or
INTELLIGENCE SUMMARY.
(Erase heading not required.)

Instructions regarding War Diaries and Intelligence Summaries are contained in F. S. Regs., Part II. and the Staff Manual respectively. Title pages will be prepared in manuscript.

Place	Date July 1916	Hour	Summary of Events and Information	Remarks and references to Appendices
	24		Sorting out connections in M.N.P. Dug outs in burrow again. Party left for VII Corps for instruction in one of Fullerphone. Making out correct diagram of all lines in area	
	25		113 Bde: take over new area on right	
	26		3 Bdes in line. Communication established by tupton & telegraph	
	27		Office arrives to go over lines for 20 Div. Every O.K.	
	28		Handing over to 20 Div by degrees. Overland of wagons loaded	
	29		Closed Office at Couin. Rejoined at Buro at 10.0 am. Company moved off at 7.45am arrived 8.45 am	
	30		Clerk Parade 10.0 am. Preparing for move	
	31		Company moved from Buro at 2.30 am for Doullens station (South) entrained at 7.15 am. arrived at Anguns at 3.45pm. detrained unloaded to Esquilbecq arriving 11.30 pm. Closed office at Buro 6.0 am crossponed at Esquilbecq same hour.	

J.W. Hemans Major
O.C. 38th Signal Co. R.E.

Signals Vol 9

Confidential.   Original.

War Diary
of

38th (Welsh) Divisional Signal Coy.

August. 1916.

Army Form C. 2118.

WAR DIARY
INTELLIGENCE SUMMARY.
(Erase heading not required.)

Place	Date	Hour	Summary of Events and Information	Remarks and references to Appendices
	1/8/16		Regulating lines new area	
	2/8/16		Visual signalling class for beginners starts. Fitting up office re-arranging wires.	
	3/8/16		Visual signalling class as above.	
	4/8/16		Advanced course for visual signallers begins. Class as above.	
	5/8/16		Cable attachment under Lieut Davis practice cable laying.	
	6/8/16		Church Parade 9-am	

Army Form C. 2118.

WAR DIARY
or
INTELLIGENCE SUMMARY.
(Erase heading not required.)

Instructions regarding War Diaries and Intelligence Summaries are contained in F. S. Regs., Part II. and the Staff Manual respectively. Title pages will be prepared in manuscript.

Place	Date	Hour	Summary of Events and Information	Remarks and references to Appendices
	7/8/16		Visual classes as on 6th. H.Q. as a/o 1A Section south moved to FORT MADYCK bathing parade return same evening	
	8/8/16		Visual signalling class as above. 1B Section H.Q. 1 and 2 Reliefs route march as above	
	9/8/16		Visual signalling classes as above.	
	10/8/16		Do.	Some lines overhauled.
	11/8/16		Visual signalling classes as above. 25 men inoculated against typhoid.	
	12/8/16		Do. Do.	
	13/8/16		Inspection of Motor cycles, bicycles, horses, harness, wagons, & billets.	

T2134. Wt. W708-776. 500000. 4/15. Sir J. C. & S.

Army Form C. 2118.

WAR DIARY
or
INTELLIGENCE SUMMARY.
(Erase heading not required.)

Instructions regarding War Diaries and Intelligence Summaries are contained in F. S. Regs., Part II. and the Staff Manual respectively. Title pages will be prepared in manuscript.

Place	Date	Hour	Summary of Events and Information	Remarks and references to Appendices
	14/8/16		Visual signalling classes as on 12/5.	
	15/8/16		No. Ons. & 1B Sekon. mule march to FORT MADYCK taking horse return evening. Visual signalling classes as usual.	
	16/8/16		Remainder of Coy. mule march as above. V.S. classes as usual.	
	17/8/16		Classes as usual.	
	18/8/16		Do. Do. 2/Lt. Maclean, 3 N.C.O's & 5 men to H Div. to assist laying cable scheme. Lieut. Davies & party 1 N.C.O. & 6 men to 29 Div. to assist laying cable scheme	
	19/8/16		Advanced parties with instruments proceed to H Div. under Capt. Bacon. Preparation for wire to [?] Visit to Sales Gate test point advanced report centre	
	20/8/16		Capt. Bacon taking over laying operation in new area. distributing centre.	

WAR DIARY
or
INTELLIGENCE SUMMARY.
(Erase heading not required.)

Army Form C. 2118.

Place	Date	Hour	Summary of Events and Information	Remarks and references to Appendices
	21/8/16		Signal office closed at ESQUELBECQ at 10 a.m. reopened at S.SIXTE at same hour. Company marched off at 6-45 a.m arrived S.SIXTE 2 p.m.	
	22/8/16		Fitting up Office changing plugs, lineman out on route	
	23/8/16		Exchange telephone exchange for repair. Continued burying cable 'G' in forward area.	
	24/8/16		Party burying 'G' line. Continued 'G' burying	
	25/8/16		Visited all Bdes. Signal officers.	
	26/8/16		2/Lt Sholam & party of 8 men proceed to TROIS-TOURS Chateau to change out-lines forward.	
	27/8/16		Church Parade 9-30 a.m. Billets lines & bicycles inspected.	
	28/8/16		2/Lt Davies E.S. promoted to Temp Lieutenant dated 20th May 16.	
	29/8/16		Reconstructing lines from ADR & Div H.Q.	
	30/8/16		Burial cable forward continues.	
	31/8/16		TROIS-TOURS. Burying through spares to Div H.Q. Office. Laying up lines at Chateau	

J.C.Humeau Major R.E.
O.C. 38th Div. Signal Co R.E.

Vol 10

War Diary
38th Signal Coy. RE
September 1916

Army Form C. 2118.

WAR DIARY
or
INTELLIGENCE SUMMARY.
(Erase heading not required.)

Instructions regarding War Diaries and Intelligence Summaries are contained in F. S. Regs., Part II. and the Staff Manual respectively. Title pages will be prepared in manuscript.

Place	Date	Hour	Summary of Events and Information	Remarks and references to Appendices
	1.9.16		All gas helmets inspected – Spare lines to TROIS TOURS. Looking plotting through – All lines clear.	
	2nd		Cpls. Motor Cycles, Lorry, Car, Three Lorries pullets inspected. Third Army lines strengthened WANT – Two men reported for duty for completion of 2nd Army Signaling Course.	
	3rd		Capts. Bacon and Self N.C.O.'s for instruction in Gas Helmets and Respirators. All Div. Gas School. All lines clear – Strengthening lines to ½ 22.	
	4th		Under line clear – Left Pole – Sant. Holland came noisy. Neutrine route in progress under Capt. Bacon – Corps Buried Scheme. 3 pipes dug – Workparties on return of gun boats. Men for Corps Buried Scheme cancelled. Improving Artillery lines	
	5th		Do.	
	6th		Do.	
	7th		Do.	
	8th		Gas Helmets inspected – Buried Scheme Works dug.	
	9th		Lorry proceed to supply Col. Scheme Spring repaired	

WAR DIARY
or
INTELLIGENCE SUMMARY.
(Erase heading not required.)

Army Form C. 2118.

Place	Date	Hour	Summary of Events and Information	Remarks and references to Appendices
	9th		Buried Cable 200 yds dug	
	10th		Church Parade - NCO & 12 men arrived from Engr Depot - all lines clear - 11 pioneers B.G. Coy R attached to "Out dig 6" for duty.	
	11th		Test argent - pt Buried Cable scheme cited - R.A. lines taken up by 11 pioneers. Buried Scheme 200 yds dug + 80 covered - Lt Perry sick.	
	12th		Lt. Lewes attached from 2nd Army.	
	13th		Line from A.D.C. to T.M. near Oluis Ghene 350 yds dug. Exercise of horses unauft. 9am - R.A. bugger line down fixed. Covered their through - Buried Scheme 200 yds dug - covered	
	14th	Hooge	Exercise of horses 11am. Lewes - Nightline from 22 to Right. Base - Buried telephone 350 yds dug New Levies 16 to 15 Bn.	
	15th		Gas Helmet Respirators inspected - Exercise of horses under Lieut Perry - Working party to turn ends cabling cancelled.	
	16th		Two men arrived from Signal Dept. - Permanent Buck	

WAR DIARY
or
INTELLIGENCE SUMMARY.
(Erase heading not required.)

Army Form C. 2118.

Instructions regarding War Diaries and Intelligence Summaries are contained in F.S. Regs., Part II. and the Staff Manual respectively. Title pages will be prepared in manuscript.

Place	Date	Hour	Summary of Events and Information	Remarks and references to Appendices
	17th		Lines as of yesterday – Buried scheme cancelled – Church parade. Motor cycles, cycles, bus, lorry, rollers inspected – Buried scheme lies pit in trench.	
	18th		Lecture on Musketry Discipline by A.M. – Inspection of plane carriers – Buried Scheme.	
	19th		Exercise of lines in morning – Run – 1/2 cable reels up forward of 1/22 – Buried Scheme. Inspection of trench filled in.	
	20th		Exercise of lines morning. Run – Cleaning up HQ line forward of HQ2 – Buried Scheme 450 yds dug 36 to dug – late start.	
	21st		Buried Scheme as above – Buried Scheme 240 yds – orderly laid Cleaning of lines – new working party.	
	22nd		Gas Helmets, ropes repairing tins inspected – two men from Signal Depot arrived – Renewed line to left Bde. – Buried scheme.	
	23rd		150 yds dug – evening reinforcing trench. R.A. lines broken – strengthened – Buried scheme 300 yds dug filled in 340 yds reinforced. Corps conference.	

WAR DIARY
or
INTELLIGENCE SUMMARY.
(Erase heading not required.)

Army Form C. 2118.

Place	Date	Hour	Summary of Events and Information	Remarks and references to Appendices
	24th		Major G.W. Stevens proceeding on leave - kept known cables only. Command of Company. - Buried scheme 300 yds aug, 350 yds laid in Heringhe.	
	25th		Repairing line from 2/86 to Left Bn. - Buried cable scheme 300 yds aug.	
	26th		Line from 2/86 continued - Buried cable 350 yds aug.	
	27th		Line as above continued - line from O.M.L. to 2/22 Essex prepared.	
	28th		O.M.L. to 2/22 work continued. Buried cable scheme 30 yds aug - Dugouts enlarged.	
	29th		Gas Helmets Resperators inspected - Buried cable scheme 60 yds aug. Lt. E.H. Davies to 10- figures for duty.	
	30th		Corps Signals conference - Buried cable scheme 35 yds aug.	

N.G.Park
for Capt. R.E.
O.C. 38th Div Signal Coy.

Secret. Vol II   Confidential

Original
War Diary - October - 1916.

Signal Company.   Royal Engineers
38th (Welsh) Division

31-10-1916.

Army Form C. 2118.

WAR DIARY
or
INTELLIGENCE SUMMARY
(Erase heading not required.)

Instructions regarding War Diaries and Intelligence Summaries are contained in F. S. Regs., Part II. and the Staff Manual respectively. Title Pages will be prepared in manuscript.

Place	Date	Hour	Summary of Events and Information	Remarks and references to Appendices
ST. SIXTE	Oct 1/16	—	Work recommenced on Horse Standings, bricks being obtained to replace the wooden standing at present in use. Cable burying work continued working from Right of Div. front to Left flank.	
	2			
	3			
	4			
	5			
	6			
	7			
	8			
	9		A permanent 4 arm 28 wire lines from Div. to join the new Corps system.	
	10			
	11			
	12			
	13		Corps Buries system continues.	
	14			
	15			
	16			
	17			
	18			
	19			
	20			

Army Form C. 2118.

WAR DIARY
or
INTELLIGENCE SUMMARY
(Erase heading not required.)

Instructions regarding War Diaries and Intelligence Summaries are contained in F. S. Regs., Part II. and the Staff Manual respectively. Title Pages will be prepared in manuscript.

Place	Date	Hour	Summary of Events and Information	Remarks and references to Appendices
ST. SIXTE	OCT 1916 21. 22 23 24 25		Work carried out in strengthening lines within area from Div to the forward exchanges. Repair work done on lines damaged by shrapnel. Weather.	
	26 27 28 29 30		Work carried out in strengthening lines within area from Div to the forward exchanges. Repair work done on lines damaged by shrapnel. Weather.	
	31		Work continues on hose standings. Cable buried system continued.	

for O.C. 38 Div Sig Coys R.E.

2449 Wt. W14957/M90 750,000 1/16 J.B.C. & A. Forms/C.2118/12.

Vol 12

Original

War Diary

November 1916

38th Divisional Signal Coy

Royal Engineers

WAR DIARY or INTELLIGENCE SUMMARY

Army Form C. 2118.

(Erase heading not required.)

Instructions regarding War Diaries and Intelligence Summaries are contained in F. S. Regs., Part II. and the Staff Manual respectively. Title Pages will be prepared in manuscript.

Place	Date	Hour	Summary of Events and Information	Remarks and references to Appendices
ST. SIXTE.	Nov. 16	10.5	Work on horse standings etc. Cpl's Buies bath system continues.	
		7ᵃ	2/Lt R.J. Dawson 3/6 Norfolk Rgt T. joins from 2nd Army School Camp.	
		11ᵃ	Major G. Stevens resumes command of Company.	
		13ᵈ	Erecting dugs strengthening lines. Making new routes for forward area.	
		15ᵈ	Making new routes for forward area	
		19.00	Corps Buies bath system continues.	

2449 Wt. W14957/Mgo 750,000 1/16 J.B.C. & A. Forms/C.2118/12.

Army Form C. 2118.

WAR DIARY
or
INTELLIGENCE SUMMARY
(Erase heading not required.)

Place	Date	Hour	Summary of Events and Information	Remarks and references to Appendices
	24th May/16		Lieut. W. Maclean R.E. joins for duty as extra one Officer.	
	28th		Building new tr. way track to 119A Rd (ELVERDINGHE CH^d).	
	29th		Do.	
	30th		II Lieut. R.F. Durrox proceeds to Corps Wireless School G.H.Q. for course of instruction in wireless telegraphy.	
	31st		Corps Buried cable system continued.	

J. Hettemans
O.C. 38th Div: Signal Co. R.E.

Army Form C. 2118.

WAR DIARY
or
INTELLIGENCE SUMMARY.
(Erase heading not required.)

Instructions regarding War Diaries and Intelligence Summaries are contained in F.S. Regs., Part II. and the Staff Manual respectively. Title pages will be prepared in manuscript.

Place	Date	Hour	Summary of Events and Information	Remarks and references to Appendices
ST SIXTE	1916 13th Decr		Locations of Division and Infantry Brigades as follows:-	
			Divl. H.Qrs. - Convent Camp ST SIXTE Sheet 28. A.1.d.1.3.	
			113 Infy Bde - CANAL BANK Sheet 28 C.19. C.4.3.	
			114 " " - CANAL BANK " 28 C.25.d.2.4.	
			115 " " - CAMP "D" " 28. A.30.6.1.3.	
	14th		Lieut W.G. POOK to H. Qrs Signal Company 39th Division relieves the 38th Division.	
			Divl H.Qrs closed down at ST SIXTE at 11 am on 14th and opens at the same hour at ESQUELBECQ.	
	15th		Divisional Signal School opened at KIEKEN PUT FARM map reference Sheet 27 N.W. C.30.d. 35 80.	
			Bath Signallers of the 113th and 114th Infantry Bdes. accended at Divisional Signal School, also as many men of the Brigade Sections as can be spared. Instruments were obtained from Divl Signal Company and Batteries. All divisional Artillery Signallers accended at Signal School.	

WAR DIARY

INTELLIGENCE SUMMARY

(Erase heading not required.)

Army Form C. 2118.

Place	Date	Hour	Summary of Events and Information	Remarks and references to Appendices
	Dec 27th 1916		Lieut B.D. PEAKE R.E. joins from 3rd Army Sig Coy Authority A.G.S./C. a/16301 dated 16/12/16.	
	2/st		Capt E.F. BACON R.E. proceeds to "E" Corps Sig C.R.E. authority A.G.S./C. a/16301 dated 16/12/16. Capt M.B. REID R.E. joins from 16th Divl Signal Bn. S. Lieut B.D. PEAKE R.E. proceeds to "E" Corps Sig C.R.E. authority VIII Corps a/3449 dated 26/12/16.	
	28th			
	29th		Major G.W. HEMANS I.A. proceeds to join 39th Divn. S. authority O/G G.H.Q. a/1244 dated 24-12-16. Lieut G.A.C. WALKER 4th L. Inniskilling Fus. joins for duty. Capt M.B. REID R.E. takes over command of Company. Signallers at 1/1st Dep Station Infantry Signallers are relieved at Signal School by Signallers of 1/5 Duke Seafield + Infantry Signallers less Signallers of 10th Scots.B.	
	30th			

W. Ruthie
Capt R.E.
Signal Co. C.R.E.

O.C. Sig 38th Divn
Capt R.E.
Signal Co. C.R.E.

Secret

Original
War Diary
38th Signal Co RE

January 1917

WAR DIARY
or
INTELLIGENCE SUMMARY.
(Erase heading not required.)

Army Form C. 2118.

Place	Date	Hour	Summary of Events and Information	Remarks and references to Appendices
ESQUEL-BECQ DIV HQ	1st Jan.		Locations of Division and Infantry Brigades as follows:— Div. HQ ESQUELBECQ 113 Bde Camps D.E. Paris 114 Bde POPERINGHE 115 Bde BOLLEZEELE	
		10/1/16	Divisional Signal School at KIEKEMPUT FARM - sheet 27 N.W. C.30.d.38.50. closed down.	
	15/1/16		38th Division relieved 36th Division in Left Sector of 8th Corps.	
St SIXTE	17/1/16		Locations as follows:- Div. Hdqrs. Convent St SIXTE sheet 28 A1.d.1.3. 113 Bde. C.19 C.43. 114 " C.25.d.2.4 115 " ELVERDINGHE. B.14.b.15.20. One Brigade of 55th Division located at Camp D. Party of 150 men provided by Res Bde for work on Dairy cattle.	
	A11.17 G.1.17.		Capt. R. Watkins buried from TROIS TOURS to ELVERDINGHE. Lieut R. Watkins from 9th Corps Signals Joined. T.W.P. CHAINE RE from 34th Div Signal Joined Weather cold and frosty.	

Kitchley C H McE
Major, O.C. D Signals

Secret

Vol 15

Original War Diary

38 Signal Co R.E.

38 Division

February, 1917.

Secret

Army Form C. 2118.

WAR DIARY
or
INTELLIGENCE SUMMARY.

38th Divisional Signal Coy.

Place	Date	Hour	Summary of Events and Information	Remarks and references to Appendices
St SIXTE	February 1917		Divisional H.Q. — Couvent De Sete A1 d 1.3 Sheet 28 NW Belgium	
			113 Inf Brigade — " " E 19 C. 4. 3	
			114 — " — E 25 d 3.4 —	
			115 — " — B 14 b 6. 10. 20 —	
			Cable burying party of 250 men provided by Pioneers N/26th Welsh bur	
			Completes the route of 40 pairs between Trois Tours and Elverdinghe Chateau	
			and also continuing with another route from Elverdinghe to A 24 C 5.5.2	
			where it will connect with Corps permanent route system.	
			The weather during the included part of the month has been	
			cold and frosty which allowed many of the labour units to apply —	
			2 Feby — Lt A H Jervis R.E. departs to join the Royal Flying Corps —	
			22 Feby — 114 Brigade moves its HQs to D Camp. A 30 Central. The 113 Brigade	
			extended its front and taken up the H.Q's vacated by 114th R.H.A. at C 20 d 2. 4	
			The remainder of the 114 Bde front being	

Army Form C. 2118.

Instructions regarding War Diaries and Intelligence Summaries are contained in F. S. Regs., Part II. and the Staff Manual respectively. Title Pages will be prepared in manuscript.

WAR DIARY
or
INTELLIGENCE SUMMARY

(Erase heading not required.)

— 9th Div. Ag Coy

Place	Date	Hour	Summary of Events and Information	Remarks and references to Appendices
St Sixte	Feby 1917		being taken over by our Right Flanking division —	
	12th / 18		The Centre and Right Group Artillery (Divisional) amalgamated into one Group with its H.Q. at Poperinghe. The necessary depend re-arrangements consequent upon the above hand over were satisfactory carried out —	
	1st March 1917			

MacRae
Capt R.F.E
for O.C. Ag 85th Division

Vol 1. Secret.

Original War Diary

March 1917.

38th Signal Co. R.E.

WAR DIARY
INTELLIGENCE SUMMARY.

Army Form C. 2118.

38th Divl Signal Co. RE

Place	Date	Hour	Summary of Events and Information	Remarks and references to Appendices
ST SIXTE	March 1917 12th		Locations of Division and Infantry Brigades as follows:- Divl HQs – CONVENT ST SIXTE A.14.13. Sheet 28 N.W. 113th Infantry Bde – C.35.a.2.4 " " 114th Infantry Bde – A.30 Central " " 115th Infantry Bde – B.14.b.15.1 " " Training of Battalion Signallers at Divl Signal Service continues. Training consisting of Visual Signalling, Telephone Signalling Telephone &c.	
	15th		2nd Lieut. W.L. Dawson (3/6 Royal Fusiliers Regt) proceeds to II Anzac Corps Signals for duty.	
	19th		The 113th Infantry Bde. move into new area at BOESINGHE being relieved by the 68th Infantry Brigade. Divl HQs to "D" Camp A.30. Central. All Battalion Signallers of the 113th Infantry Brigade were sent through a close course of instruction	

WAR DIARY
or
INTELLIGENCE SUMMARY.
(Erase heading not required.)

Army Form C. 2118.

Place	Date	Hour	Summary of Events and Information	Remarks and references to Appendices
	29th		in the area of the former Brigade as amplifies.	
			Formation of Entire Area Signal Section formed from Brigade and Headquarters Sections.	
	30th		114th Infantry Brigade relieved by the 113th Infantry Brigade the former going into rest training area at BOLLEZEELE.	

M. Mid
Major R.E.
Comdg 38th Divn Signal Coy

Secret

Vol 2

Original
War Diary April 1917

38 Signal Co R.E.
38th Division

30/4/17

Army Form C. 2118.

WAR DIARY
or
~~INTELLIGENCE SUMMARY.~~ 39th Div. Sig. Co.
(Erase heading not required.)

Instructions regarding War Diaries and Intelligence Summaries are contained in F.S. Regs., Part II. and the Staff Manual respectively. Title pages will be prepared in manuscript.

Place	Date	Hour	Summary of Events and Information	Remarks and references to Appendices
ST. SIXTE	April 1917 10th		Locations of Divisional Infantry Brigades as follows:—	
			Divisional Headquarters CONVENT, ST. SIXTE	
			113th Infantry Brigade — c.25.d.2.4 Belgian Sheet 28 N.W.	
			114th " " A.30 Centre " "	
			115th " " B.14. Centre " "	
			Training of Battalion Signallers at Divisional Signal School continues. Training consisting of Visual, Telephone, Telephone &c.	
	14th		No Centre Area Signal Section ceases to exist. Personnel returns to Brigade Signal Sections &Os. 39th Division takes over the Centre Sector.	

T2134. Wt. W708-776. 5000 9/16. 4/15. Sir J.C. & S.

WAR DIARY
INTELLIGENCE SUMMARY
(Erase heading not required.)

Army Form C. 2118.

Place	Date	Hour	Summary of Events and Information	Remarks and references to Appendices
	22d		1 Sec Infy Bde. relieved 114th Infy Bde in the Lancashire Farm Section, the relief with HdQrs at Camp A 30. Central.	
	25th		Two Lieuts. A.J. Robertson R.E. & J.S. Stennett R.E. join for duty from Second Army Signal Coy.	
	29th		Headquarters 114th Infantry Brigade move to ELVERDINGHE	

Unwin
Major R.E.
Comdg. 38th Divil. Signal Coy R.E.

Secret.

Original War Diary
May. 1917.

Signal Coy. Royal Engineers
38th (Welsh) Division.

31. 5. 1917.

WAR DIARY of 39th Div Signal Coy RE

Army Form C. 2118.

INTELLIGENCE SUMMARY.
(Erase heading not required.)

Instructions regarding War Diaries and Intelligence Summaries are contained in F.S. Regs., Part II. and the Staff Manual respectively. Title pages will be prepared in manuscript.

Place	Date	Hour	Summary of Events and Information	Remarks and references to Appendices
ST SIXTE	May 1917			
	1st		Location of Divl HQrs and Infantry Brigades are as follows:-	
			Divl H.Q. — Corner St. Sixte A.1.d.1.3 Elven Sqre S.W. 28 N.W.	
			116th Infy Bde — CANAL BANK B.19.c.3.4 "	
			117th " " — ELVERDINGHE B.4.6.6.1 "	
			118th " " — BOULEZEELE A.44.C. Swine Regmt. Sh. 4bis Sht. 24	
	2nd		Laying of Battalion Signallers at Divl Signal School continue. Laying Party erecting of visual (?) telephone Buzz/Buzz telephone &c.	
	3rd		Training carried out by Brigade in regard to Airplane contact Party, Pigeons, Power Buzz &c, in which Signal Sections Egpt Repl. Corps Murns W/T have contributed in formed units.	

WAR DIARY
INTELLIGENCE SUMMARY.
(Erase heading not required.)

Army Form C. 2118.

Place	Date	Hour	Summary of Events and Information	Remarks and references to Appendices
	18th		115 A Inf Bde relieves 114th Inf Bde	
	19th		114th Inf Bde relieves 113th Inf Bde in the front line	
			Jam Section with Bryce runs into the HERZEELE - HOUTKERQUE area.	
	20th		Divn HQrs & their Signal Sections of 113 Bryce in reserve area consisting of Bryce Coranto Stakes Schele &c.	

1/9/17

Maurice Swaety Capt
O.C. 38th Divl Sig Coy

Sec'd

Onginne
War Diary
38th Div Signal R E
June 1917

30/7/17

Army Form C. 2118.

WAR DIARY
or
INTELLIGENCE SUMMARY. 38th Div Signal Coy
(Erase heading not required.)

Instructions regarding War Diaries and Intelligence
Summaries are contained in F.S. Regs., Part II.
and the Staff Manual respectively. Title pages
will be prepared in manuscript.

Place	Date	Hour	Summary of Events and Information	Remarks and references to Appendices
ST SIXTE	June 1916 1st		Locations of Divisional Headquarters, Infantry Brigades etc:— Div H.Q. — CONVENT ST SIXTE M.1.A.1.3 Sheet 28 N.W. 113th Infantry Brigade — QUELMES near Shirley 114th Infantry Brigade — CANAL BANK C.19 C.4.9 Sheet 28 N.W. 115th Infantry Brigade — ELVERDINGHE B.14.C.13.1. Sheet 28 N.W.	
	2nd		Training of Battalion Signallers at Div: Signal School continues. Ongoing sprouts of refreshers yr Signal Telephone Power Buzz, D III Telephone Lucas Lamps & C.	
	3rd		Training carried out by Brigade in reserve at QUELMES Signalling of Brigades carried out Station Schemes wanted.	
	4th		Lucas Lamps to & c. Lieut (A/Capt) J.H. Chalmers wounded for Base Hospital to England.	

WAR DIARY
or
INTELLIGENCE SUMMARY.
(Erase heading not required.)

Army Form C. 2118.

Place	Date	Hour	Summary of Events and Information	Remarks and references to Appendices
	10th		Divisional Headquarters move from St SIXTE to VOX VRIE Camp A.15.a 4.8 Sheet 28 N.W. Divl Report Centre closes at ST SIXTE at 4pm re-opens at VOX VRIE Camp at 4.30 same day. Completion of course at Divl Signalling School	
	11th		114th Infy Brigade relieved by 113th Infy Bde in the LANCASHIRE FARM Section, the former moving to T.14.9125	
	11th 12th		rest area. 2nd Gwent Brigade relieves the 115 th Infy Bde in the BOESINGHE Section, the later move to PROVEN	
	21st		Lieut (Wegn) Palmer R.E. posted from 16th Divl Sigs for duty i/c O/o of 38th Divl Artillery Signals	
	29th		38th Division relieved by 29th Division. The former moving to NORRENT FONTES training area Divl Hq Divl Close down at VOX VRIE camp 12 noon & re-opens at NORRENT FONTES	
			Temp/Lt Col Comdg 38th Divl Signal Coy	

Secret

Original War Diary

38th Signal Co. R.E.

38th Division

July. 1917

31/8/7

Vol 20.

WAR DIARY

INTELLIGENCE SUMMARY. 38th Divl Signal Coy R.E.

Army Form C. 2118.

Place	Date	Hour	Summary of Events and Information	Remarks and references to Appendices
NORRENT FONTES	July 1917 1st		Location of Divisional Headquarters and Infantry Brigades as follows:-	
			Divisional Headquarters - NORRENT FONTES. Ref: Maps	
			HAZEBROUCK SA 1/20,000	
			LENS 11 1/100,000	
			113th Infantry Brigade - FLECHIN.	
			114th do - ESTREE BLANCHE	
			115th do - LAIRES	
	2nd		Training consisting of Brigade Forward Station Scheme, Infantry Drill, Musketry, Intensive in Chielka and bad drill.	
	13th		Divisional Headquarters move from Training Area to GODESWAERSVELDE.	

WAR DIARY
or
INTELLIGENCE SUMMARY.
(Erase heading not required.)

Army Form C. 2118.

Place	Date	Hour	Summary of Events and Information	Remarks and references to Appendices
	19th		Divisional Headquarters move to PROVEN.	
	21st		38th Division relieves the 29th Division in the ZWAANHOF SECTOR with Headquarters at VOX VRIE Camp (Ref: map 1/40,000)	
	24th 28th		(Sheets 24 and 28) T/Lieut. R.J.REESE R.E. wounded by hostile shell fire Advanced Divisional Headquarters opens at ELVERDINGHE.	
	31st		XIV Corps attack with 38th Division on right. Operations hampered by rain. Communication with Brigades maintained by wireless. Great difficulty experienced in keeping lines through owing to rain. Casualties:- killed - 3 O.R. Disappeared - 1 O.R. Missing - 1 O.R. Wounded - T/2nd/Lt. J.S. HARRIS R.E. Major 76 y.o.r. 7 O.R. O.C. 38 Div. Signal Coy. R.E.	

Secret.

Original
War Diary
August 1917.
38th Signal Co. R.E.

Army Form C. 2118.

WAR DIARY
INTELLIGENCE SUMMARY. 38th Divl Signal Coy
(Erase heading not required.)

Place	Date	Hour	Summary of Events and Information	Remarks and references to Appendices
	August 1917			
	1st		Location of Divl HQrs and Infantry Brigades as follows:-	
			Divl HQ Oro - VOX VRIE Camp (Ref map 1/40,000 Sheet 28)	
			Adv. Divl HQ Oro - ELVERDINGHE B.14.b.1.1.	
			113th Infantry Bde - HUDDERSFIELD ROAD.	
			114th " - C.13.c.1.2	
			115th " - C.19.c.4.3	
	6th		Advance Divl HQ Oro closes at ELVERDINGHE. 10th Divn relieves 38th Division. Oke takes with Headquarters at PROVEN	
	7th		Training at PROVEN consisted of Cable drill Visual Signalling etc.	
	13th		Lt. A.E. COLLIS R.E. joins from Fifth Army Signal Coy for duty.	

WAR DIARY
INTELLIGENCE SUMMARY.
(Erase heading not required.)

Army Form C. 2118.

Place	Date	Hour	Summary of Events and Information	Remarks and references to Appendices
	19th		38th Divn. relieves the 20th Divn. The former with Hd. Qrs. at VOX VRIE Camp and Adv. Divl. Hd. Qrs. at ELVERDINGHE, and the latter with Hd. Qrs. at PROVEN.	
	21st		2nd Lieut. J.S. HARRIS R.E. returns from Signal Depot. Buzz from old telephone system into captured German line commenced with working parties from 20th Divn.	
	22nd		Capt. R. WATKINS R.E. to Third Army Signal Coy for duty.	
	26th		Buzz started on 21st completed and working well.	
			115th Brigade resumes the offensive in conjunction with Corps on our right. Operators hampered by rain. Communication to Brigade in the line maintained without difficulty during the action.	
	28th		2/Lt. A.G. COLSTON R.E. to 23rd Dvl. Sig. Coy for duty.	
	29th		113th Infy Bde. relieves the 115th Infy Bde. The latter withdraws to C.13. c.2.1.1. Buzz commenced from AU BON GITE to ALLOUETTE FARM. Nature of ground & quantity of shell hole rendered	
	30th			

Army Form C. 2118.

WAR DIARY
or
INTELLIGENCE SUMMARY.
(Erase heading not required.)

Place	Date	Hour	Summary of Events and Information	Remarks and references to Appendices
Both?	31st		Work difficult. 114th Inf. Bde relieves the 115th Bde. The former with Bde. HQ. at C.13.C.2.1 and the latter with its HQ. on the MALAKOFF FARM area.	

WMMead
Major RE
O.C. ap. 38th Div. Signal Co.

Secret.

Original War Diary
September 1917
38th Divl Signal Co R.E.

Army Form C. 2118.

WAR DIARY
INTELLIGENCE SUMMARY
(Erase heading not required.)

38th Divisional Signal Coy. R.E.

Vol 2

Place	Date	Hour	Summary of Events and Information	Remarks and references to Appendices
	8/9/17	10h.	Station of Divl. H.Qrs. and Infantry Brigades as follows:— Divl. Headquarters – VOX VRIE Bwo. (Ref map 1/40,000 Sheet 28) Advanced Divl H.Qrs. – ELVERDINGHE B.14.b.1.1. 113th Infy. Bde. – HUDDERSFIELD & STRAY FARM C.3.d.2.4. 114th Infy. Bde. – FUSILIER HOUSE C.13.c.2.1 115th Infy. Bde. – MALAKOFF FARM area B.22.b.3.2.	
	4/5th		114th Infy. Bde. relieves the 113th Bde. The former with H.Qrs. at STRAY FARM & HUDDERSFIELD & the latter with H.Qrs. in the MALAKOFF FARM area.	
	11th		20th Division relieves 38th Division. The former with Divl. H.Qrs. at WELSH FARM & the latter with H.Qrs. at PROVEN.	
	13th		Divl. H.Qrs. closes down at PROVEN & opens same day at ESTAIRES Sheet 36a.	

Army Form C. 2118.

WAR DIARY
INTELLIGENCE SUMMARY
(Erase heading not required.)

Place	Date	Hour	Summary of Events and Information	Remarks and references to Appendices
	16th		Lieut. A.J. ROBERTSON M.C. R.E. to England on R.O.F. One Officer & 10 Signallers from Battalions to commence attending weekly FULLERPHONE Course at Corps Signal School.	
	17th		Divn. HQrs. closes down at ESTAIRES & opens same day at CROIX DU BAC (Sheet 36) relieving 54th (West Lancashire) Division.	
	24th		Lieut. T.C.N. BOWEN R.E. joined from 2nd Army Signal Coy. for duty.	
	25th		Original Signal School assembles. NCO's & men from Batteries & Battalions, making a total of 45.	
	26th		Programme of training consists of theory Signalling, Lectures, Organization of communication in a Division, Glossary, Electricity Magnetism, D III Telephone, Buzzing, Telephone Simple Exchanges, Numerous duties, Fullerphone B.O., Wireless.	

O.C. 38th Divl Signal Coy.

WAR DIARY
or
INTELLIGENCE SUMMARY.

Army Form C. 2118.

Place	Date	Hour	Summary of Events and Information	Remarks and references to Appendices
	Oct 1917		Weekly Telephone Course at XIth Corps Signal School. Personnel employed repairing lines from Bethune as before. No 2 Mechanical Trench Diggers also are doing very good work in trenches yet the pumping gear as overall progress is being made.	

M H Morris
I Lieut RE
for OC 38th Div Signal Coy

WAR DIARY
INTELLIGENCE SUMMARY
(Erase heading not required.)

Army Form C. 2118.

38th Div Signal Coy

VI 23

Place	Date	Hour	Summary of Events and Information	Remarks and references to Appendices
CROIX DU BAC.	Oct 1914		Jenkins of Divnl Headquarters as follows:-	
			Divisional HQrs – CROIX DU BAC G.6.c.8.0 Sheet 36A	
			113th Infantry Bde – Do. H.11.a.5.4 Do.	
			114th Do. FLEURBAIX H.20.d.66 Do.	
			115th Do. ERQUINGHEM-LYS H.4.a.3.8 Do.	
			Signal Divnl Signal School continues	
			Training consisting of visual signalling, lectures	
			on organization of Comm-nications in Division,	
			Elementary Electricity and Magnetism, D III Telephone	
			Simple Exchanges, Buzzphone, Fuller Buzz's &c.	
	14th		Lieut. De Brugh 115th Bde now South West	
			Warrao China for duty at Divisional	
			Signal School.	

Army Form C. 2118.

WAR DIARY

38th Div. Signal Coy R.E.

INTELLIGENCE SUMMARY.

(Erase heading not required.)

Instructions regarding War Diaries and Intelligence Summaries are contained in F. S. Regs., Part II. and the Staff Manual respectively. Title pages will be prepared in manuscript.

Vol 24

Place	Date	Hour	Summary of Events and Information	Remarks and references to Appendices
CROIX DU BAC	Aug 1917	10 a	Location of Divisional Headquarters as follows:— Divl Headquarters — CROIX DU BAC G.6.c.90 Sheet 36 a. 113th Infy Bde — " H.11.a.54 " " 114th Do — FLEURBAIX H.20.d.66 " " 115th Do — ERQUINGHEM-LYS H.4.d.3.8 " " Signal School continues. Training at Divisional Signal Office continues. Training of Visual Signalling, Testing for organisation of commencement in Division. Elementary Exercises by Magnetism, VII Telephone Simple exercises, Telephone etc. Cable burying exercises remainder Progress is being made.	

WAR DIARY
or
INTELLIGENCE SUMMARY.
(Erase heading not required.)

Army Form C. 2118.

Place	Date	Hour	Summary of Events and Information	Remarks and references to Appendices
	20th.		Lieut. Rouse Burges Course assembles at the Divl Signal School - 12 vacancies allotted to Infantry Brigade.	
	24th.		Lieut. Signalling Course terminates at Divl Signal School. Reinforcements rejoin units.	
	26th.		Second Signalling Course assembles — Vacancies allotted as follows:— Infantry Brigades — 34 each Artillery — 30	
	28th.		Lt. Mytek 88. T.F. found for duty from Reserve Army. M. Rowbotham for OC 38th Divl Signal Coy.	

Army Form C. 2118.

WAR DIARY
or
INTELLIGENCE SUMMARY
(Erase heading not required.)

38th Divisional Signal Coy.

Vol 25

Place	Date	Hour	Summary of Events and Information	Remarks and references to Appendices
Croix du Bac	1/2/17		Location of Divisional Headquarters and Infantry Brigades as follows:— Shut 36a. Divisional Headquarters – CROIX DU BAC – 9.6.c.8.0 113th Infantry Brigade – H.11.a.5.4. 114th Do – FLEURBAIX – H.26.d.6.6. 115th Do – ERQUINGHEM–LYS – H.4.d.3.8 Training at Divisional Signal School continues. Programme of training consisting of Visual Signalling, Lectures on Organisation of Communication in a Division, Elementary Electricity Magnetism & Telephone, Simple Exchanges, telephone &c. Cable laying in forward areas continues & considerable change is being made.	

WAR DIARY
or
INTELLIGENCE SUMMARY

Army Form C. 2118.

Place	Date	Hour	Summary of Events and Information	Remarks and references to Appendices
	12/12		Lt. I.Y. Pearson RE to Signal Depot Rouen for temporary duty.	
	24/12		2nd Lieut. M. Scott (E.L.) ? for Army Signals duty from Gist Army Signals.	
	30/12		Major M. Shea M.C.I.E. to General Wireless Depot ABBEVILLE for one weeks course. Capt. Burge ? and ? Signal School on ? course consisting of Engineers from Infantry Brigades.	

M.W. Rowe Capt.
for O 38 m Div Signal Co R.E.

11/1/8

WAR DIARY
or
INTELLIGENCE SUMMARY

Army Form C. 2118.

Vol 26

Place	Date	Hour	Summary of Events and Information	Remarks and references to Appendices
Merville	12/1/18		Location of Divisional Headquarters and infantry Brigade was as follows:—	
			Divisional Headquarters — MERVILLE R.22.d.5.2	
			113th Infantry Brigade LES LAURIERS M.15 & 20.10	
			114th " " NORRENT FONTES N.15.B.4.2	
			115th " " ESTAIRES L.29.97.8	
			D⁰ D⁰ General at B.29.D.5.80	
			Signal School opened in 1918 ...	
			on Jany 18th 1918 ...	

The Signallers in the 2 Divisions
of Artillery took part in the Division-
of Manoeuvres. Through going to lay
22nd Army and Programme of
December 23rd Army and Programme of
training was laid down and is now being
carried out.

Artillery
────────
Signal Personnel carrying out
Scheme of training, Both the Artillery
Signal Officer

W.M.Lee
Major RE
OC 58th D[iv] Sig Co

11/2/18

Army Form C. 2118.

WAR DIARY
or
INTELLIGENCE SUMMARY

(Erase heading not required.)

38th Div. Signals R.E.

Vol 27

Place	Date	Hour	Summary of Events and Information	Remarks and references to Appendices
MERVILLE	Feb 1st	—	Location of Divisional Headquarters and Infantry Brigades as follows :—	
			Divisional Headquarters MERVILLE Sheet 36 t 36n K.22.a.5.2.	
			113th Infty Bde. do. LES LAURIERS K.15.c.00.10	
			114th do. do. {NORRENT FONTES N.33.B.2.2.	
			115th do. do. ESTAIRES L.29.d.7.8.	
	1st to 9th		Training of all Battalion Signallers and the whole of the Divisional Signal Coy concentrated near Vieux Berquin continues and good results are obtained, especially in the matter of liaison between R.E. and Infantry Battalions ~~Brigades~~ themselves	

Army Form C. 2118.

WAR DIARY
or
INTELLIGENCE SUMMARY
(Erase heading not required.) 38th Div Signal Co R.E.

Instructions regarding War Diaries and Intelligence Summaries are contained in F. S. Regs., Part II. and the Staff Manual respectively. Title Pages will be prepared in manuscript.

Place	Date	Hour	Summary of Events and Information	Remarks and references to Appendices
	Feb 9th		Signal School at E.29.d.25.80 closes down. Signallers returned to their Units. Only No.1 Section remains. Training is continued especially in horsemastership.	
	16th		38th Division relieves the 57th Division with Headquarters at STEENWERCK A.17.d.5.4 The Corps Buried Cable system continues. It was found that little progress had been made with the Corps Buried Cable scheme since the area was taken from this Division just before Christmas. The left and Centre Brigade areas have most of their main circuits buried but about 800 – 9000 yards of trench has still to be dug to make communication in these areas at all secure.	

Army Form C. 2118.

WAR DIARY
or
INTELLIGENCE SUMMARY

(Erase heading not required.)

3rd Div. Signal Coy R.E.

Place	Date	Hour	Summary of Events and Information	Remarks and references to Appendices
	Feb 16th		In the Right Brigade area, practically the whole system has yet to be laid down. Not much labour is available and progress is very slow. A party from Div. Signal Coy is working with about 100 men. A cable section from XV Corps is working in the Centre Brigade Area, with a party of about 100 men every other day. In the Left Brigade area a party of Div. Signal Coy. is working with occasional labour on small technical jobs. The Wireless system is good but at present lack of equipment is a very serious disadvantage.	
	19		No. 5 Section of the Divisional Signal Coy. is authorized and application made to transfer the necessary Battalion Signallers	

WAR DIARY
or
INTELLIGENCE SUMMARY

Army Form C. 2118.

Place: 30th D.V. Signal Coy R.E.

Date	Hour	Summary of Events and Information	Remarks and references to Appendices
Feb 25		A Refresher Course for R.F.A. Signallers commenced at STEENWERCK. Programme of training comprises Lamps, Flags, Discs, Buzzer & Ox test it was discovered that these men had fallen much below the standard of even 2nd Class signallers, thereby showing the great necessity for frequent refresher courses during trench warfare.	

M.W. Rowe Capt.
for O.C. 30th D.V. Sig Coy R.E.

Army Form C. 2118.

WAR DIARY
INTELLIGENCE SUMMARY.
(Erase heading not required.)

36 Div Signal Coy R.E.

Vol 28

Place	Date	Hour	Summary of Events and Information	Remarks and references to Appendices
STEENWERCK	March		Location of Divisional Headquarters and Infantry Brigades as follows:-	
			Divl. H.Qrs. STEENWERCK M3 a.f A.17.d.5040	
			113th Inf. Bde - ERQUINGHEM " H.14.d.40.70	
			114th " " - ARMENTIERES " B.29.c.50.00	
			115th " " - ERQUINGHEM " H.11.a.45.40	
	2nd		2/Lt. E.J.CASTELLO, R.F.A. from 168 R.F.A. Brigade E to be O i/c 121 Brigade Signal Sub Section.	
	13th		Capt. J. POLAND, R.E. admitted to C.C.S. sick.	
	19th		Lieut. F.Y. PEARSON, R.E. rejoins unit from Signal Base Depot on completion of temporary duty.	
	22nd		Major M.B. REID, M.C. R.E. evacuated to C.C.S. Wounded (Gas).	

WAR DIARY
or
INTELLIGENCE SUMMARY.

Army Form C. 2118.

Place	Date	Hour	Summary of Events and Information	Remarks and references to Appendices
	26.4.		Major E.J. ASTON, M.C. R.E. from 30 Corps Signals assumed temporary command of Company vice Major M.BREID, M.C.R.E	
	29.4.		Capt. R.G. HARKING M.C. R.E from 26th D.H.Q. for attachment vice Capt. J. POLAND, R.E. R.F.A. Signallers attached for instruction return to units.	
	3/0.4		10th Division relieved by 34th Division, the former with H.Q at MERVILLE. —

15th Corps front scheme was continued especially in the High Houses area where the new huts were exceedingly unsatisfactory. Progress was not very rapid owing to scarcity of labour. The work was very much interrupted from the 9th March onwards owing to the expectation of a possible German attack. on 15th Corps front. A good many emergency offices had to be fitted up units | |

WAR DIARY
or
INTELLIGENCE SUMMARY

Army Form C. 2118.

were continually changing positions at short notice. The Section was employed during the last fortnight of the month on the construction of the Cable Hd. of the Division at LE KIRLEM which was completed before the Division was relieved.

From the 14th to 24th all were Obvs [Observers] forward of Bde HQ. were were continuously and the tests gave excellent results.

Great attention was paid to the Visual Scheme as the number of Strongholding Stations necessary consequently a large number of Personnel had to be employed. In connection with the running of these Buzzer no Amplifier Scheme gave most valuable results. During the latter part of the month there was a great deal of theory showing all over the Div. Front. The new Buzzer system worked excellently

WAR DIARY
INTELLIGENCE SUMMARY
(Erase heading not required.)

Army Form C. 2118.

Place	Date	Hour	Summary of Events and Information	Remarks and references to Appendices

but the red system in the Night. He was was frequently broken. The absolute necessity of having at least one main route back to Div. H.Q. was demonstrated by the difficulty which would have been experienced with Regimental routes only as these were invariably cut. Regimental runs ERQUINGHEM was were often broken by Long range gun fire as far back as CROIX DU BAC.

M.H.Thorne
for O.C. 38th Divl Sig Coy R.E.

V.Corps.
Third Army.

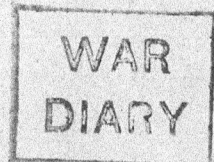

38th DIVISIONAL SIGNAL COMPANY, R.E.

A P R I L

1 9 1 8

April 1918   **WAR DIARY**
or
INTELLIGENCE SUMMARY.
(Erase heading not required.)

Army Form C. 2118.

38th Div. Signal Coy.

Place	Date	Hour	Summary of Events and Information	Remarks and references to Appendices
	1st	—	Divisional Headquarters closed down at MERVILLE and opened Headquarters at TOUTENCOURT, map ref Sheet 57D. V.I.C.60.60. Capt. R.G. LARKING, M.C. R.E. accidentally killed whilst riding a motorcycle 20th result of collision with motorlorry.	
	2-12		**Visual**, wireless and messages app messages app worked in conjunction with Brigade Signallers, been carried out in conjunction with Brigade Signallers. **Visual.** Greater use has been made of visual alternative methods of communication. Visual stations have been continuously manned and messages transmitted daily with good results. **Wireless.** Considerable attention has been given to wireless communication. Messages have been transmitted	

Army Form C. 2118.

WAR DIARY (2)

INTELLIGENCE SUMMARY.

(Erase heading not required.)

regularly by this means. Special attention has been directed to eliminating delay and little seems to have now been obtained.

Mounted D.R. work.

Owing to the to date of the war and the difficulty of obtaining access to units which were in some cases treated in rotation away from main roads it was found that motorcycles were not always satisfactory. Orderlies mounted on horseback have been used with good results.

Cable work.

Cable sections have been practice in fact laying from engines but flying rods and across country.

Since any work of this sort has been done most of the original men of the company have changed and the reinforcements from the base are of course quite untrained. Our progress was not...

D. D. & L., London, E.C. (A8001) Wt. W1771/M2031 750,000 5/17 Sch. 52 Forms/C2118/14

WAR DIARY
INTELLIGENCE SUMMARY

(Erase heading not required.)

Army Form C. 2118.

(3)

Place	Date	Hour	Summary of Events and Information	Remarks and references to Appendices
	8.			
	10.		Lieut. R.H. Bage M.C. R.F.A. evacuated "gassed". Capt. E.A. MAGUIRE, M.C. R.E., joined as O/c 38th Div. Arty. Sigs. During rest, Relief from the Division was under orders to move at short notice and was for 48 hours at an hours notice only. Stores to be kept packed up and wagons loaded as this together with the very bad weather prevented extensive training.	
	12.		Div. Headquarters closed TOUTENCOURT as 7 am and opened at CONTAY map ref. Sheet 57d. U.21.c.40. (about Centre). Location of Infantry Brigades and Y.C.H.R. as follows:— Left Brigade W.21.c.60 Sheet 57d. Right Brigade E.2 Central " " Reserve Brigade HENENCOURT V.24.d.53 Sheet 57d. Y.C.H.R. V.13.c.6.7 Sheet 57d. Roads (above) In order to save all horses and villages as much as possible completely new reports centre were	

Army Form C. 2118.

WAR DIARY
or
INTELLIGENCE SUMMARY.
(Erase heading not required.)

(4)

Place	Date	Hour	Summary of Events and Information	Remarks and references to Appendices

establish in a copse on high ground and this
received a large co-operative fire. the
point was well seen to all targets that Infantry
and Artillery ws attacked as seem up, all
telegrams were either sent by means of wireless. The
A.W.R.A. exchange was situate close by.
after the rest system was established, considerable
amount of work was received which resulted
being employed on "running through
a large number of men
it.

On 22nd 113th Infantry Brigade attacked on left sector in conjunction
with 35th Division on our left and 39th advanced about
150 yards. All live lines behind Brigade Report Centre
just to the South West of BOUZINCOURT kept well as
there was very little back shooting but forward of these,

WAR DIARY
INTELLIGENCE SUMMARY

Army Form C. 2118.

despite a very heavy "Indirect Cable" communication by telephone was impossible after the first hour or so. The ladder was repaired at any-rate but it was cut wherever the enemy barrage came down. Some wagons with ammunition were brought forward of our Brigade. Behind the Rise they were not used as there was no need of them.

On 26th the Right Brigade front was taken over by the 2nd Aust. Div. and the Brigade went to the Reserve.

Brigade were withdrawn to TOUTENCOURT and HERRISART. As a result of this a good class Horse was needed up. He wished Training was also to be carried on. He strove to have fallen ranks up. Signalling appears to have been given no last set was anything was needed to the Brigade from 38 Div Sig Cy

WAR DIARY
INTELLIGENCE SUMMARY.

Army Form C. 2118.

38th Div. Sconce Off Vol 30

Place	Date	Hour	Summary of Events and Information	Remarks and references to Appendices
	May 1918 1st		Location of Divisional Headquarters and Infantry Brigades as follows:- Div. Hqrs - CONTAY Mgy. U.21.c.4.0. Sheet 57D. 113 Inf. Bde. - V.4.c.80.90. Sheet 57D. 114 Do - V.4.c.90.90. " 115 Do - V.15.a.5.0. "	
	2.5.		Training in wiring, wireless, and runners. 28 Cooks courses and gas schools obtained. Cadre Schemes were practiced in for laying from wagons back along road and a reconnaissance and gas progress was made.	
	6.9.		Divl. Hdqs. closed 12 noon 6 May at CONTAY and reopened same hour at TOUTENCOURT. V.16.60.60. Sheet 57D.	

WAR DIARY
— or —
INTELLIGENCE SUMMARY.
(Erase heading not required.)

Army Form C. 2118.

Place	Date	Hour	Summary of Events and Information	Remarks and references to Appendices
	10th		During this time great use was made of visual as wireless was not often. Communication was again out by this method. Visual Stations were continuously manned and messages transmitted daily with excellent results. Cable burying by infantry in the forward area was continued under the supervision of Signal Service Personnel and 1 reels were obtained. Work was carried out in constructing a new dugout at XA Visual Station (and Pwk. Station.) 1/4 th Infantry Brigade attacked the enemy positions on the high ground near AVELUY WOOD and was	

Army Form C. 2118.

WAR DIARY
or
INTELLIGENCE SUMMARY.
(Erase heading not required.)

Instructions regarding War Diaries and Intelligence Summaries are contained in F. S. Regs., Part II. and the Staff Manual respectively. Title pages will be prepared in manuscript.

Place	Date	Hour	Summary of Events and Information	Remarks and references to Appendices
	1-19		a slight advance. They were unable to consolidate and were obliged to retire to their original line. Telephone communication was maintained all the time, as there was not was not required. It was found this reinforcements received from the Base were not up to the standard required and during this period a certain amount of sickness occurred amounting to a rite of physical training incurrence out.	
	20/31		38th Division relieved by 35 Division on 20 May, the former with HQ & quarters at HERISSART. Owing to Period in reserve extensive training was carried out by all Sections of the Company.	

Army Form C. 2118.

WAR DIARY
or
INTELLIGENCE SUMMARY.
(Erase heading not required.)

Place	Date	Hour	Summary of Events and Information	Remarks and references to Appendices

Training was carried out on the following lines:—
7 – 8 am – Physical training rifle exercises
9 – 12.30 pm – Lectures, lectures, musketry returns visual and wireless.

2.30 pm – Firing practice on rifle range.
Sports on a company basis were held. Judges awarded to the winners of various competitions.

A Show turn-out Competition Parade altogether was held as was hoped on the following points:—
1. Condition of horses
2. Condition of harness & saddlery
3. Cleanliness turnout, jumpers
4. General condition of horses & harness.

Army Form C. 2118.

WAR DIARY
or
INTELLIGENCE SUMMARY.
(Erase heading not required.)

Place	Date	Hour	Summary of Events and Information	Remarks and references to Appendices
	5/6		Smartness of personnel in open drill. Erection of clothing, personal equipment. Judges were Colonel Bennett, OC. Rue Train, and Lieut. Colonel Dainters, ADSignals V Corps. The Prize was awarded to "C" detachment after a close contest.	

M.W.Hope
Capt.
for O.38th Divl Sig Coy S

WAR DIARY

INTELLIGENCE SUMMARY. 38th Divl. Signal Coy R.E.

(Erase heading not required.)

Army Form C. 2118.

Place	Date	Hour	Summary of Events and Information	Remarks and references to Appendices
	1-26		Location of Divisional Headquarters and Infantry Brigades as follows:-	
			Divl. HQ. - HERISSART	See France 57D
			113th Infy. Bde. - RUBEMPRE	" " "
			114th " " - TOUTENCOURT	" " "
			115th " " - HERISSART	" " "
			Training was carried on the following lines:-	
		9am-9.12.30	Physical training, rifle exercises, Lectures, Lectures mostly instruction as weird rendles.	
		2.H.30	Firing practices on rifle range	
			38th Division relieves 63rd (RN) Division on 5th with Headquarters at map ref. O.22.a.1.6. See France 57D.	

WAR DIARY
INTELLIGENCE SUMMARY.
(Erase heading not required.)

Army Form C. 2118.

Place	Date	Hour	Summary of Events and Information	Remarks and references to Appendices
			A Divisional Signal School of instruction formed at MAISON PONTHIEU (Lieut. Lewis II). The class was divided for instruction as follows:- (a) 1st class Signallers - Refreshers and Adv. Course (b) do " " - For Classification as 1st class Signallers. (c) New men for training as signallers. Changes were allotted as follows:- R.3.A. - 1 Officer + 35 other ranks 113 Bty Bde - 3 Officers + 69 " " 114 " " - 2 " 40 " " 115 " " - - 39 " " The instruction was chiefly for the following lines:- Appliance, Aldis Lamp Buzzer. Map reading Morning waves Stationary & Working.	

Line lying in trenches
4 + 3 Company
connecting up running withouts etc etc.

A message came out on the enemy position
by a Battalion of the 113th and 115th Brigades. They
gave their objectives but found their movements
by the enemy.

During this operation communication in the Division
was very further were cut.

Most of the communication in the Division
was sent out by wave and wireless as a
considerable number of messages were transmitted
during this period
by these methods

WAR DIARY
INTELLIGENCE SUMMARY

The C.R.P.S. buried cable system continues and considerable progress was made. Considerable attention to the evening system has to be made to make sure we to be sure of the buried system as to run the main commencing of running off permanent routes.

Word of Rear Corps Heartes able wg was laid Outside of Sew Junts as also from Bugle Grand Signal Offices. These wg connects to terminal boards. This was the means of cleaning all local cables from running into dugouts.

10 pairs on the R-H.L wing were found through to 10 pairs of HL-S and buried at HL. Sets were taken off S of these pairs and brought on to terminal board at HL.

A new August was made at F Westpunt (Q.19.a.8.20)

All detachments were fully occupied during this Show in setting up all spare lines up in use. Work was Rumours concerning enemy to airmen in the Company caused by is "evidence of P.V.O." and quite a number knew to to be colour.

Promoted by Service in the Field - King's Birthday Honours Gazette dated 3rd June 18 -

23381 A/CSM. R.TAIT.
D.C.M.

Mention in despatches in the Supplement to the London Gazette dated 20th May 18 : -

Major   M.B. REID. M.C.
Lieut.   E.A.G. WALKER M.C.
2 Lieut. J.S. HARRIS RE
6294   L/Cpl J. HORNE

WAR DIARY
or
INTELLIGENCE SUMMARY.
(Erase heading not required.)

Army Form C. 2118.

Instructions regarding War Diaries and Intelligence Summaries are contained in F. S. Regs., Part II. and the Staff Manual respectively. Title pages will be prepared in manuscript.

Place	Date	Hour	Summary of Events and Information	Remarks and references to Appendices
	June 30		Awarded Meritorious Service Medal in the Supplement to the London Gazette dated June 17th 18 — 63937 S/Cpl JC FORBES.	
			Signals to Byses Grovals who placed on the new Corps Buzz from S-VF Shes giving Communication from Division unspire Barles on the buzy, with the exception of 450 yards from our exchange to LS test Point.	

M W Rouse
Captain
ADO, 38th Div Signal Coy

Army Form C. 2118.

WAR DIARY
INTELLIGENCE SUMMARY
(Erase heading not required.)

38 Div Signal Co R.E.   WW 32

Place	Date	Hour	Summary of Events and Information	Remarks and references to Appendices

	July 1918 1-15		Locations of Divl Hqrs and Infantry Brigades as follows
			
			Div Headquarters O22 d.1.6 Sheet 57D.
			113th Inf Brigade P27 a.95.15 do.
			114th do do P24 c.1.3 do.
			115th do do P24 d.3.4 do.
			
			Night 14/15. Cable bury. Working party consisted of 1500 Infantry assisted by Signal Service personnel. Bury was completed from 114th Brigade to Deep Dugout at P36 o 1.9 approximately, with the following exceptions:-
			
			     A. About the last 100 yards outside P36 a 1.9
			
			     B. 35 yards of trench dug but not filled in at P30 o 7.7.
			
			It was an exceptionally dark night, and rather wet, and the Infantry had great difficulty in digging.	

Army Form C. 2118.

WAR DIARY
or
INTELLIGENCE SUMMARY.
(Erase heading not required.)

Place	Date	Hour	Summary of Events and Information	Remarks and references to Appendices
	19/31		38th Division relieved by 17th and 63rd Divisions. Locations as follows:-	
			Div Headquarters .... O 22 d 1.6 Sheet 57 D.	
			113 Inf Brigade P 27 a 95.15 do.	
			114 do. TOUTENCOURT. do.	
			115 do. HERISSART. do.	
			Whilst in reserve extensive training was carried out by the Signal Company. The following classes were held:-	
			Battalion Signallers Course	
			Cable Section and No 5 Section Linemans Course	
			Advanced Lineman's Course	
			Brigade Section Lineman's Course	
			Training was chiefly carried out on the following lines:-	

Batty Signallers Course

1. Jointing.
2. How to superimpose telephone and fullerphone with bridging coil.
3. How to test with Q and 9 (a) bells (b) lines etc.
4. Simple faults on 4 plus 3, fullerphone and D III, and how to remove them.
5. General talk on stores.
6. How to change over working wires.

Cable Section and No 5 Section Linemans Course

1. Pole climbing with and without climbers.
2. Rest dry joints in 40 lb bronze and 60 lb G I.
3. Practice in quick repair of route when wires only are broken.
4. Practice in building suspended cable.

WAR DIARY
or
INTELLIGENCE SUMMARY.
(Erase heading not required.)

Army Form C. 2118.

Place	Date	Hour	Summary of Events and Information	Remarks and references to Appendices
			5. Principles of testing with Q & I detector.	
			6. Practice in finding faults.	
			7. Jointing a bunch of D5's, brass quad & 7 pair bronze etc.	
			8. Duties of Linemen at Buried Cable Test Points.	
			9. Lengthy practice in procedure for mending a broken bury of various types of cable.	
			Advanced Linemen Course.	
			1. Pole climbing with and without climbers.	
			2. Best dry joints in 40 lb bronze, 60 lb G.I. heavy copper and iron wires.	
			3. Quick repair of a route when wires only are broken.	
			4. Methods of running a suspended cable along a permanent route.	

Army Form C. 2118.

WAR DIARY
or
INTELLIGENCE SUMMARY.
(Erase heading not required.)

Place	Date	Hour	Summary of Events and Information	Remarks and references to Appendices
			5. Principles of revolving and crossing and how to recognise their existence.	
			6. How to test for contact between pairs.	
			7. Testing out with 2 Test Sets and no phones.	
			8. Jointing bunch of D5's bravo quad, and 7 pair bravo.	
			9. Buried Cable. Amount of average task. Method of paying off various cables, including practical work with armoured quad and 7 pair bravo. Various methods of crossing obstacles. Marking of buried routes. Methods of jumpering etc.	

Brigade Section Linemans Course.

1. Principles of testing with a Q-I detector.
2. Practice in finding faults.
3. Picking up a speaking circuit.
4. Jointing lunch of D5's, brass grad and 7 pair brass.
5. Duties of linemen at Buried Cable Test Points.
6. Lengthy practice in procedure for mending a broken line of various types.
7. Practice in leading in to terminals boards and wiring of small offices.
8. Short general lectures on care of instruments, and simple faults, laying of buried cables, overhead and trenches, and on what constitutes a good lineman.

Army Form C. 2118.

WAR DIARY
or
INTELLIGENCE SUMMARY.
(Erase heading not required.)

Place	Date	Hour	Summary of Events and Information	Remarks and references to Appendices
			A Power Buzzer – Amplifier and Loop Set course for Brigade Power Buzzer Section also was held. Three signallers from each Brigade attended.	

J.W. Rowe
Major
for O 38th Div Sig Co R.E.

38th Div. Signal Co. R.E.

August 1918. Army Form C. 2118.

WAR DIARY
or
INTELLIGENCE SUMMARY.
(Erase heading not required.)

Place	Date	Hour	Summary of Events and Information	Remarks and references to Appendices
4ug.	1 Aug		Hd. Qtrs. Leativillers; 113th Bde Toreville; 114th Bde Toutencourt; 115th Bde Heressart	
	2 Aug		Inspection. An inspection of the Personnel transport of the Signal Co. was made by the Divl. Commander — who expressed his satisfaction at the appearance of the men and the condition of the horses.	
			Competition. A competition was held between Nos 2, 3 & 4 Sections in speed & accuracy in transmitting messages by means of Runners, Power Buzzers, Lamps, Fullerphones and DIII Telephones over a distance of 3000 yards. The scheme was exacting and the results most instructive.	
			Visual. Special attention was given whilst the Division was in rest to improve this method of communication in the event of open warfare and a considerable improvement was effected	

38th Sigl. Signal Co. August 1918. Army Form C. 2118.

WAR DIARY
or
INTELLIGENCE SUMMARY.
(Erase heading not required.)

Place	Date	Hour	Summary of Events and Information	Remarks and references to Appendices
			Wireless. Special efforts were made to improve communications by this method whilst the Divn. was in rest. The maximum number of stations were manned but it was found difficult to cope with lengthy messages owing to the delay caused by the necessity of using cyphers.	
	6 Aug		The Division relieved the 17th Divn in the Avelay Sector. Division HQrs. remained in the same place, but communications were switched over without much trouble. During the next fortnight no men were available as digging parties, but a considerable amount of work was done by the Company on the existing system, renewing and strengthening test points and bringing the records up to date. The latter meant a great deal of work as the existing records were hopeless, but the wisdom of this ordering of men time and labour was amply proved by later events. Too much attention cannot be paid to records + general tidiness in test points	

38th Dn Bde. C.R.E. August 1918. Army Form C. 2118.

WAR DIARY
or
INTELLIGENCE SUMMARY.
(Erase heading not required.)

Instructions regarding War Diaries and Intelligence Summaries are contained in F. S. Regs., Part II. and the Staff Manual respectively. Title pages will be prepared in manuscript.

Place	Date	Hour	Summary of Events and Information	Remarks and references to Appendices
			as well as the selection of really good men to take charge of them. Power Buzzers. During this period Power Buzzers working from Battalions to advanced Brigade gave excellent results. Quite a large number of messages were sent by this means, and if telephonic communications had been broken they would have proved very valuable indeed. Loop Sets were used from R.S.A. O.P's to Bde. H.Qrs. Communication was good and reliable, but it does not appear that wireless will ever be of much assistance to Observation Officers.	
	15 Aug		About the 15th Aug reports from all sources showed that an enemy retirement was probable and the Dvn. on our left made some slight advance, eventually gaining a foothold on the southern slope bank of the Ancre, just north of Thiepval. The Dvn. on our Right made through Albert.	
	21 Aug		On the night of the 21/22nd the Dvn. attacked by moonlight. One Bde. went over in a S.Easterly direction. On the extreme left of the Dvn. sector. The other 2 Brigades passed through Albert formed up on the extremely narrow frontage between the flooded river the Albert - Bapaume road attacked in a North Easterly direction. There was thus a gap of 3,000 yards

30th Div. Sig Coy RE.   August 1918.

WAR DIARY or INTELLIGENCE SUMMARY
Army Form C. 2118.

Place	Date	Hour	Summary of Events and Information	Remarks and references to Appendices
			Where no attack took place the line was not established again continuously till a depth of 4000-5000 yards had been reached. A large number of prisoners were thus cut off & captured. During the next ten days the Divn. advanced by bounds. Very heavy fighting took place but almost every attack was successful despite the extreme exhaustion of the troops. Communications were established on the following general scheme. Infantry Bdes & F.O.B's each ran out one pair of light cables as they advanced while Divl. cable sections pushed a main setting of two pairs of heavy field cable as far as Bde. Forward stations. The two lines were used continuously by the Staff for Telephone work & yet the number of telegrams was very large, anything between 700-1000 per day. Superimposing was therefore essential except by sounder or Fullerphone. The length of the telegrams, the number of addresses were beyond all our previous experience. Interim reports & operation orders were often 250-300 words long, the number of telegraphists was quite insufficient to clear with the continuous traffic. Steps have however been taken to cut this down. The C.R.A. lived at Bn. H.Q. Light field communication through these 2 forward lines, but this was not	

38th Divl. C.R.S.   August 1918

5

WAR DIARY
or
INTELLIGENCE SUMMARY

Army Form C. 2118

(Erase heading not required.)

Place	Date	Hour	Summary of Events and Information	Remarks and references to Appendices
			Found to be satisfactory & after the first few days he moved with the support or reserve Inf. Bde. & had direct lines to most of his groups. As the result of experience it had been decided that 2 lines forward are not sufficient & in future 3 will be run as far as the support Bde. from there One line being put straight through to each Bde. the odd sections used as Bde. laterals. An offshoot of the Div Sigs will live at the support Bde. to ensure an equal share of the laterals, lines to all, and to control the system generally. Wireless now need a certain amount both between Div. & Bdes. between Divn. and the Corps, but owing to the length of the telegrams their secret nature which necessitates cipher, it was not found to be of much use for urgent work. Visual work was however done between Bde. signal stations and Bdes. by Lucas lamps. None Bruggers were noticed. Visual moves of Divn. and Bdes. usually took place late in the evening and consequently communication could not be established owing to the night coming on. It was therefore not of much use. Mounted D.Rs There were found most necessary to carry all D.R.L.S messages. Officers grooms had been	

383rd Duty C.R.E. August 1918

WAR DIARY
or
INTELLIGENCE SUMMARY
(Erase heading not required.)

Army Form C. 2118.

Place	Date	Hour	Summary of Events and Information	Remarks and references to Appendices
			were used for this purpose, but they required a map reading into a great drawback.	
			Runners were not found necessary behind Bois.	
			Pigeons. The birds took approximately one hour to home the message took nearly 2 hrs after that to reach Divl.H.Q. A few messengers got back but the supply of birds was extremely limited & the infantry did not make the best use of them.	
			Message Carrying Rockets were not used.	
			On the whole communication was good the greatest difficulty experienced was the breaking of existing lines by so much traffic passing frequently. "Army" calls had to work. The cable supply forbade more lines, but if there had been 2 lines to each Bde HQ perhaps they would hardly have been sufficient. An elaborate system cannot be made during moving warfare & the staff must comply with the necessary restrictions.	
24 Aug			Adv. Div. JHQ opened at Hedauville. 25th Aug. Advanced Div. Class in Sedauville. trespans at Nova Redoubt	
26 Aug 30 Aug			Adv. Div. Class at Nova Redoubt. Central stores opened at Albert.	

M.W. Rowe
To O.C. 383rd Duty Eng. Coy

D. D. & L., London, E.C.
Wt. W1771/M2931 750,000 5/17 Sch. 52 Forms/C2118/14

Army Form C. 2118.

WAR DIARY
or
INTELLIGENCE SUMMARY.
(Erase heading not required.)

War Diary -
September 1918.

3d Div Signal Co R.E.

WO 34

WAR DIARY
INTELLIGENCE SUMMARY.

Place	Date	Hour	Summary of Events and Information	Remarks and references to Appendices
High Wood Sq 8.8	1st		Ref Map Sheet 57C/NW00 Ref Map Sheet 57C/NW00 Morval and Sailly-Saillisel Division attacked Morval and Sailly-Saillisel Two attacking Bdes and Div HQ at T9A2u near Guillemot Reserve Bde Guinchy. It was found during earlier operations that the C.R.P. required further use of one line forward from div HQ in order to save cable it was decided by the G.O.C. that the two leading Bdes should have their HQ together whenever possible and that the C.R.P. should place his HQ at the double Bde HQ. One officer of No. 1 Section was placed in charge of this combined signal office, having under him the four divisional operators normally attached to the Bdes and one cable detachment. Great difficulty was experienced in maintenance	

WAR DIARY
or
INTELLIGENCE SUMMARY.

Army Form C. 2118.

Place	Date	Hour	Summary of Events and Information	Remarks and references to Appendices
LES BŒUFS	3		Owing to shortage of men - through sickness there only 18 out of 30 sweepers were available for work. 1 Officer and 12 Signallers from the Pioneer Bn. collecting cable in the back areas.	
	4		Division HQ moved to dug outs at Les Bœufs. Two leading Bdes and CRA in dug outs 1000 yds E of Morval. Res Bde at Guinchy. Two leading Bdes and DA HQ moved to Sailly Saillisel and Res Bde to a site 1000 yds north. Later in the day the Res Bde moved to a dug out in the sunken road V.10.d.6.7. The DA HQ remaining with the support Bde. Two DA lines were laid from Sp/Bde to new position of line Bde. Several hours at night locating a fault in one	

WAR DIARY
or
INTELLIGENCE SUMMARY.
(Erase heading not required.)

Army Form C. 2118.

Place	Date	Hour	Summary of Events and Information	Remarks and references to Appendices
	4 (cont'd)		of the lines. Caused by the time in a Dt Cable completely breaking the insulation. The same trouble has been experienced twice since then.	
	5	0300	Div. relieved by 21 Div. A small party of operators linesmen was left to run the Div HQ office at Les Boeufs. The remainder of HQ Coy moved back to Old Div. HQ at High Wood to refit.	
	5		Repairing, refitting, reeling up cable. Owing to shortage of linesmen it was found necessary to attach operators from Div Bath Week detachment and about Nos Section.	
	11		Div relieved 17 Div in the line.	
Étricourt	11		HQ Étricourt, two Leading Poles 7TA near Guid P35.d 8.3	

WAR DIARY
or
INTELLIGENCE SUMMARY.

Army Form C. 2118.

Place	Date	Hour	Summary of Events and Information	Remarks and references to Appendices
Res Bde Forn Wurdo Farm P31.D9.8	11 (cont²)		Work on improving huts & picking up cattle.	
	12/6		Owing to shelling Div H.Q. moved from huts into dug-outs in the Canal Bank.	
	17		Div "D" moved to Camp at O36.d.3.7 Two wire lines RA HQ moved to Battn HQ, E of Poeasenthook 102.d.1.8.	
	17		An Adv Div Sig Office was established at P35.D.8.3. Three D8 cables were laid from this point to the leading Bde H.Q. During the night the area of the double Bde HQ was very heavily shelled with gas. Lance Cpl Jenkins Spr Bok awarded M.M. for repairing over 50 breaks in 4 hours whilst wearing gas masks	
Elverdinghe				

Army Form C. 2118.

WAR DIARY
or
INTELLIGENCE SUMMARY.
(Erase heading not required.)

Place	Date	Hour	Summary of Events and Information	Remarks and references to Appendices
(contd)			under very heavy shell fire	
	16		Div. attacked Boyeaucourt.	
	20		Div relieved by 7 Div	
	21		Div HQ moved to Camp 036 D 3.7	
			One Bde Rocquigny	
			One Bde Le Translot	
			One Bde Fun Wuds Farm P31 c 9.8	
	21		Refitting and reeling up cable	
	6		A short course was held for one signaller per Batt'n.	
	28		and Battery in instruments.	
			A Div School was formed at Bde Camp for 12 men per Batt'n RFA & Bde in operating telephones duties	
			duration one month.	
			Div Batt'y Signallers commenced a course in	

WAR DIARY
or
INTELLIGENCE SUMMARY.

(Erase heading not required.)

Army Form C. 2118.

Place	Date	Hour	Summary of Events and Information	Remarks and references to Appendices
	28 16 30		C.W. W/T at Div Hq. School. Div HQ moved to VISC near Noel le Grand. Odeo Party concentrated in Heudecourt Area. Two pairs of DD Cables were laid to Railway Embankment nr Epehy Station with a view to subsequent operation. General. Wireless DS at HQ continuously manned. Each Bde was equipped with one TS one pair of loop sets, of which rear set was continuously warned and 2 power buzzers, but the latter could not be used owing to difficulty of transport.	

Army Form C. 2118.

WAR DIARY
or
INTELLIGENCE SUMMARY.
(Erase heading not required.)

Instructions regarding War Diaries and Intelligence Summaries are contained in F. S. Regs., Part II. and the Staff Manual respectively. Title pages will be prepared in manuscript.

Place	Date	Hour	Summary of Events and Information	Remarks and references to Appendices
General			Trial behind Boles was a failure owing to shortage of men and difficulty in picking up stations in the dark	

Army Form C. 2118.

WAR DIARY
or
INTELLIGENCE SUMMARY.

(Erase heading not required.)

Place	Date	Hour	Summary of Events and Information	Remarks and references to Appendices
			Casualties	
			Wounded 14	
			Sick 13	
			Total 27	
			Reinforcements 13	
			Hons Awards 5 { 1 military cross / 4 " medals	
			C.J. Aston	
			Major. R.E.	
			O/c 38 Divl Signal Co. R.E.	

Instructions regarding War Diaries and Intelligence Summaries are contained in F. S. Regs., Part II and the Staff Manual respectively. Title pages will be prepared in manuscript.

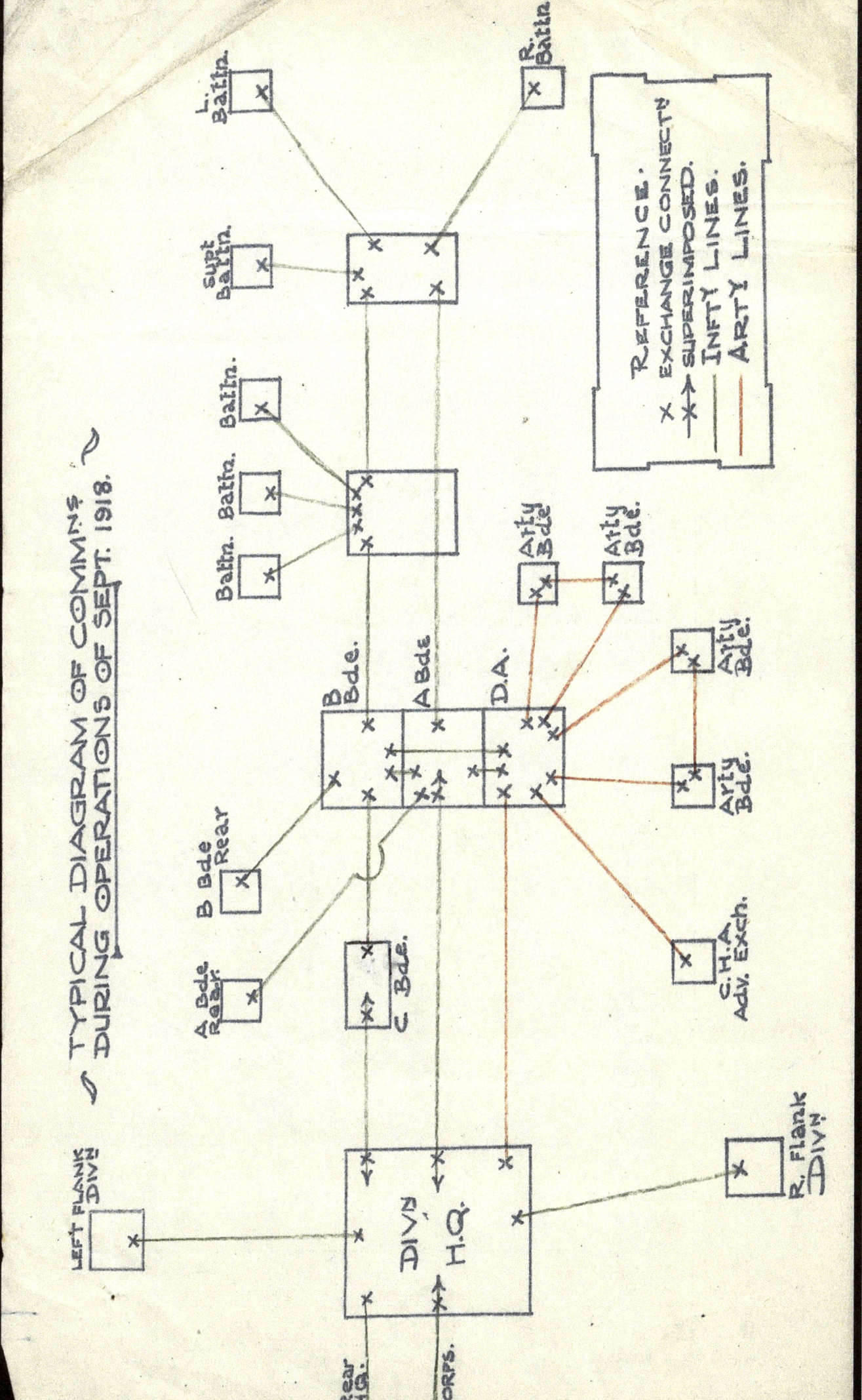

WAR DIARY
or
INTELLIGENCE SUMMARY.

Army Form C. 2118.

WD 35   38th Div Signal Co. R.E.

Place	Date	Hour	Summary of Events and Information	Remarks and references to Appendices
Hea. FINS.	2nd		Div. Report Centre at EPEHY was withdrawn.	
	3rd		Div. Report Centre re-established at EPEHY. One pair of cables from DivnHQ to Report Centre.	
	4th		Div Report Centre established with 50th Div. at DUNCAN POST west of GUILLEMONT FARM. One pair of cables from EPEHY to Report Centre. 113th Bde. moved to EPEHY. Report Centre cable via Report Centre cable. 115th Bde. moved to BONAY. One pair headless laid from 113th Bde. Exchange to 115th Bde.	
EPEHY.	5th		On night 4/5th 113th & 115th Bdes took over left of line. held by 50th Div – Divnl Report Centre H.Q. BONAY. Communications – one pair from DivnHQ to BONAY. Div Aux Exchange opened at RICHMOND QUARRY. S.28.a.8.8. Sheet 57 B – One pair cables laid from EPEHY to this exchange.	

(A2001) D. D. & L., London, E.C. Wt. W1777/M2031 750,000 5/17 Sch. 53 Forms/C2118/14

Army Form C. 2118.

WAR DIARY
or
INTELLIGENCE SUMMARY.
(Erase heading not required.)

2/

Instructions regarding War Diaries and Intelligence Summaries are contained in F. S. Regs., Part II. and the Staff Manual respectively. Title pages will be prepared in manuscript.

Place	Date	Hour	Summary of Events and Information	Remarks and references to Appendices
	Oct 18			
HINDENBURG LINE.	6th		113th & 115th Bde HQrs moved to S.28.d Sheet 57 B - Two Bns Cables laid from these two Bdes to RICHMOND QUARRY.	
	7-8th		Div HQ moved to S.21 Central (HINENBURG LINE)	
			Div attacked - attack successful - Communications kept throughout the attack.	
	9th		33rd Div passed through 38th Div & continued the advance at 05.20 hrs.	
VILLERS OUTREBUX.	10th		Div HQ moved to VILLERS OUTREAUX.	
BERTRY	11th		Div HQ moved to CLARY.	
CLARY	12th		Div HQ moved to BERTRY	
	14th		Div relieved 33rd Div in the right sector of the Corps.	
			Div HQ - TROISVILLES	
			Signal Bde - TROISVILLES	
			Reserve Bde - BERTRY	
			The Rest of Cables to each Bde Lateral from line to Support Bde.	

Army Form C. 2118.

WAR DIARY
or
INTELLIGENCE SUMMARY.
(Erase heading not required.)

3/

Place	Date	Hour	Summary of Events and Information	Remarks and references to Appendices
	15-18		Work on improving & laying Cables	
	19th		Div. Report Centre established at TROISVILLES. Two Pairs Cables laid from TROISVILLES to double Box HQ at K.35.d. and continued forward to Bakn. HQ in view of pending operations.	
	20th		At 02.00 hrs Div. attacked	
	22nd		On night of 22nd/23rd 33rd Div relieved 38th Div in the line 38th Div HQ moved to chigants K.25.d.4.4.	
K.25.d.4.4.	24th		38th Div HQ moved to MONTAY.	
MONTAY & RICHEMONT	25th		38th Div HQ moved to RICHEMONT	
	26th		Div relieved 33rd Div in the line at 16.00 hrs New main route of two Pairs cables forward was laid to Beles and the old route which ran down to BAVAI road reeled up.	

Army Form C. 2118.

WAR DIARY
or
INTELLIGENCE SUMMARY.

(Erase heading not required.)

Place	Date	Hour	Summary of Events and Information	Remarks and references to Appendices
			H	
	24-31		Great difficulty was experienced maintaining lines owing this period owing to very heavy knowing fire.	
			Casualties during month :-	
			Killed - 3	
			Wounded - 14	
			Evacuated to hospital - 23	
			Reinforcements - 17	
			Recruiting - 1 Militiaman McCaul	
			Anderson Lieut. R.E.	
			for O.C. 38th Div. Signal Coy R.E.	

Ipswich and 113 Bde
" 114 " " 114 "
" 115 " " 115 "
C. Richardson
D. A.

BM 1573
19/10/18.

Attachment to Signal Arrangements
for 20-10-18.

1. **Dropping Station.**

   One additional dropping station has been arranged at Advanced Bde Hqrs. K.25.d.7.4. Duplicate messages will be dropped there and at the Troisvilles station which is at P.4.b.8.8.

2. **Wireless.**

   The Tanks have wireless communication as follows (by C.W.):—

   Between O.C. Tanks at Div. H.Q. and a station at K.25.d.7.4.*

   Also between either of these stations and a Tank used by Div. Observers.

   Div. observers also have a Forward Loop Set communicating to Bde Hqrs. at K.25.d.7.4. If necessary via one of the Forward Loop Sets with Battalions.

3. A Telephone line is also laid to the Balloon at Bertry Stn.

* O.C. Tanks arranging to have this station in the vicinity of K.25.d.7.4.

[signature]
Major R.E.
O.C. 38 Div. Sig. Co.

19-10-18.

Army Form C. 2118.

WAR DIARY
or
INTELLIGENCE SUMMARY.

33rd Division Signal Co[mpany]

(Erase heading not required.)

Place	Date	Hour	Summary of Events and Information	Remarks and references to Appendices
RICHMONT	Nov 1918 1st		Preparing communications for impending operations.	
	2nd		All three Infantry Brigades and Divn Report Centre moved to ENGLEFONTAINE.	
	3rd		Communications — Two pair Kerles from Divn to Report Centre. One pair from Report Centre to each Infantry Brigade. Great difficulty was experienced in maintaining communication owing to the very heavy hostile artillery & M.G. fire.	
ENGLEFONTAINE A.H.Q.			Our Headquarters move to Englefontaine. Division attacked to FORET DE MORMAL. Attack a complete success	

D. D. & L., London, E.C.
(A800) Wt. W1771/M2031 750,000 5/17 Sch. 32 Forms/C2118/14

Army Form C. 2118.

WAR DIARY
— or —
INTELLIGENCE SUMMARY.
(Erase heading not required.)

Instructions regarding War Diaries and Intelligence Summaries are contained in F. S. Regs., Part II. and the Staff Manual respectively. Title pages will be prepared in manuscript.

Place	Date	Hour	Summary of Events and Information	Remarks and references to Appendices
	5th		33rd Division forces through the Division and continues to advance.	
LOEQUIGNOL	6th		Our Headquarters move to LOEQUIGNOL. Divn. in close support of 33rd Division.	
	7th		Infantry Brigade moves forward to SARBARAS.	
	8th		Divn relieves 33rd Division. Our Headquarters - AULNOYE. One Brigade - AULNOYE. Two Brigades - POT DE VIN.	
AULNOYE	9th		Communications - one Rail cables to each Brigade. Divn. attacks and advances up to the AVESNE-MAUBEUGE Road.	
	10th		Enemy found to have retired during night 9/10. Leading Brigade pushes forward to the River SOLNE.	

(AB001) D. D. & L., London, E.C. Wt. W1771/M2031 750,000 5/17 Sch. 53 Forms/C2118/14

WAR DIARY
or
INTELLIGENCE SUMMARY.

(Erase heading not required.)

Army Form C. 2118.

Place	Date	Hour	Summary of Events and Information	Remarks and references to Appendices
	11th		Hostilities ceased 11.00 hrs. VI Corps took over my duties of advance guard on whole of this Army front but an outpost line was maintained by 56th Leaving Brigade.	
	30th		Cleaning and painting wagons. General overhaul and checking of stores. Roing and driving drill.	
	29th		Ten men of Company proceeded to England for employment as miners. Casualties &c during month. Wounded — 7. Evacuated Sick — 25. Reinforcements — 22. Honours & Rewards — 3 Military Medals. 1 Bar to Military Medal.	H.O. Division Signal Coy for OC 38th Divisional Signal Coy

WAR DIARY or INTELLIGENCE SUMMARY

Army Form C. 2118.

38th Div. Sig. Coy.
Dec. 1918.

Place	Date	Hour	Summary of Events and Information	Remarks and references to Appendices
AULNOYE	10th- 24th		Educational Classes arranged within the Company in the following subjects:- Electrical Engineering — 8 Students Electricity & Telegraphy — 14 " Shorthand — 13 " Bookkeeping — 8 " French — 31 " Gaelic — 8 " Mathematics — 20 " All men were attached from units of the Div. to attend these courses.	
	26th		Advance Party sent by lorry to GLISY to arrange communications for the Division	

Army Form C. 2118.

WAR DIARY
or
INTELLIGENCE SUMMARY.

2.

(Erase heading not required.)

Instructions regarding War Diaries and Intelligence Summaries are contained in F. S. Regs., Part II. and the Staff Manual respectively. Title pages will be prepared in manuscript.

Place	Date	Hour	Summary of Events and Information	Remarks and references to Appendices
	26.		Which was moving here on the 31st Oct. Parties sent out to salve Aigrue Stores.	
	29.		Transport left for GLISY by march route taking five days.	
INCHY.	30.		Divisional Headquarters move to INCHY.	
GLISY.	31.		Divisional Headquarters move to GLISY. Casualties re during month:— Admitted to hospital sick — 18. Officers demobilized — 32. Reinforcements — 12.	

Henderson Lieut.
for O.C. 38th Div Sig Coy.

D. D. & L., London, E.C.
Wt. W1771/M2031 750,000 5/17 Sch. 53 Forms/C2118/14
(A600.)

WAR DIARY
or
INTELLIGENCE SUMMARY. (Erase heading not required.)

Army Form C. 2118.

38th Div. Signal Coy.

January 1919

VM 38

Place	Date	Hour	Summary of Events and Information	Remarks and references to Appendices
GLISY.	1-14.	—	Continuation of Educational Classes and Ordinary of Signal duties	
QUERRIEU 14th			Divisional Headquarters moved to QUERRIEU. The Signal Company remained at GLISY until the 16th so as the Camp at QUERRIEU was not ready. Educational Classes started in December & continued throughout the month. A survey of all permanent works within the Division was carried out & a map prepared so that the Division could decide what works they wished to purchase, & what works could be delivered.	

Army Form C. 2118.

WAR DIARY
or
INTELLIGENCE SUMMARY. 2

(Erase heading not required.)

Instructions regarding War Diaries and Intelligence Summaries are contained in F. S. Regs., Part II. and the Staff Manual respectively. Title pages will be prepared in manuscript.

Place	Date	Hour	Summary of Events and Information	Remarks and references to Appendices
	29.		Cable cahode parties were organized within Division. About 100 miles of various sorts of field cable below during the month. 22 horses sent for evacuation to England for sale. Personnel to Dispersal Camps for demobilization commenced not — 2 off. — 5 offrs — 29 OR. Rewards for Services in the Field — New Years Honours Gazette 1919 — DCM — 1 MSM — 5 Mentions — 6. Henderson Lt. Col R.E. for OC 38 Divl Sig Coy R.E	

D. D. & L., London, E.C.
(A8001) Wt. W1771/M2031 750,000 5/17 Sch. 52 Forms/C2118/14

Army Form C. 2118.

WAR DIARY
or
INTELLIGENCE SUMMARY.
(Erase heading not required.)

February 1919   38th Div Signal Coy R.E.   WO 39

Place	Date	Hour	Summary of Events and Information	Remarks and references to Appendices
QUERRIEU	1-28		Educational Classes as under continued throughout the month.	
			Subject No of Students	
			French 18.	
			Mathematics 14.	
			Shorthand 7.	
			Wireless 6.	
			Telegraphy 3.	
			Electrical Engineering 6.	
			Signal Stores selued during the month.	
			Permanent Line 6 miles	
			Field Cable 20 miles	

WAR DIARY
or
INTELLIGENCE SUMMARY.

Army Form C. 2118.

Place	Date	Hour	Summary of Events and Information	Remarks and references to Appendices
			Personnel to Concentration Camp for dispersal:-	
			93 Other Ranks.	
			40 Horses proceeded to Dover Camp for sale and transmission to England.	
			H. Davidson Lt. R.E. for O.C. 39nd Div Sig Coy R.E.	

Army Form C. 2118.

WAR DIARY
INTELLIGENCE SUMMARY
(Erase heading not required)

Place: 38th Div Signal Coy R.E.

Date	Hour	Summary of Events and Information	Remarks and references to Appendices
March 1919			
OVERVIEW 1-31		Educational Classes as usual continued until 15th March when they were closed down owing to rapid demobilisation of students.	
		No. of Students	
		Subject	
		French — 18	
		Mathematics — 14	
		Shorthand — 7	
		Wireless — 6	
		Telegraphy — 3	
		Electrical Engineering — 6	

WAR DIARY
or
INTELLIGENCE SUMMARY

(Erase heading not required.)

Army Form C. 2118.

Place	Date	Hour	Summary of Events and Information	Remarks and references to Appendices
			The calling of Signal Officers was continued throughout the month. Personnel to Concentration Camp for dispersal. — 48 other ranks. 14 men of the Army of Occupation were transferred to the Second Army & Fourth Corps on 30 March 19.	

H Bridestein Capt R Sigs
for GO 39th Dn Sig Coy

Army Form C. 2118.

WAR DIARY
INTELLIGENCE SUMMARY
38th Div. Signal Coy. R.E.

(Erase heading not required.)

Place	Date	Hour	Summary of Events and Information	Remarks and references to Appendices
QUERRIEU	April 1919		Salving of Signal Stores was carried out in this area.	
GLISY		9.30	Divisional Headquarters closed at QUERRIEU and opened at GLISY on 7th April with a detachment of the Signal Company at BLANGY TRONVILLE. Salving and checking of stores was chiefly carried out during the period. The following Personnel left this unit for demobilization during the month. Officers — 1 O.R. — 24	

Smiling [?] Lieut. R.E.
O.C. 38th Div. Sig. Co. R.E.

Army Form C. 2118.

WAR DIARY
or
INTELLIGENCE SUMMARY
(Erase heading not required.)

38th Divisional Signal Co. R.E.

Place	Date	Hour	Summary of Events and Information	Remarks and references to Appendices
			May 1919.	
GLISY	May 1919		Location – Divisional H.Q. – GLISY Divl Signal Coy – GLISY with a detachment of Signal Company Stations at BLANGY TRONVILLE. Salving of Signal Stores and packing of Signal Stores for disposal or detachment was chiefly carried out during the month. Strength of Personnel for Machinery of demobilization was reduced by 75%. Personnel surplus to new active requirements were demobilized.	R.6

WAR DIARY
or
INTELLIGENCE SUMMARY

(Erase heading not required.)

Army Form C. 2118.

Place	Date	Hour	Summary of Events and Information	Remarks and references to Appendices
			Strength of Company on 3/5/19 - Officers 2 OR 43	

Signed
Capt.
OC 38th Div Signal Coy RE

www.ingramcontent.com/pod-product-compliance
Lightning Source LLC
Chambersburg PA
CBHW081535160426
43191CB00011B/1761